creative STAMPING in polymer clay

NORTH LIGHT BOOKS

cincinnati, ohio
www.artistsnetwork.com

creative STAMPING in polymer clay

BARBARA MCGUIRE

NORTH LIGHT BOOKS

cincinnati, ohio
www.artistsnetwork.com

about the author

BARBARA A. MCGUIRE has been creating and selling art for thirty years. Her experience with color **(AS AN OIL PAINTER)** and design **(AS A STAINED GLASS ARTIST)** laid the foundation for expression in a new and dynamic medium—polymer clay. She is the author of three polymer clay books, appears regularly on television craft shows and instructs at national shows. She is the designer of ✳ **POLYFORM'S STAMPLETS KITS** and ✳ **SHAPELETS TEMPLATES** and the developer of ✳ **CREATIVE CLAYSTAMPS DUO RELIEF RUBBER STAMPS.** Barbara lives in San Francisco, and its cultural influences are reflected in her work.

CREATIVE STAMPING IN POLYMER CLAY. © 2002 by Barbara A. McGuire. Manufactured in Singapore. All rights reserved. No part of this book may be reproduced in any form or by any electronic or mechanical means including information storage and retrieval systems without permission in writing from the publisher, except by a reviewer, who may quote brief passages in review. Published by North Light Books, an imprint of F&W Publications, Inc., 4700 East Galbraith Road, Cincinnati, Ohio 45236. (800) 289-0963. First edition.

Other fine North Light Books are available from your local bookstore, art supply store or direct from the publisher.

06 05 04 03 02   5 4 3 2 1

Library of Congress Cataloging-in-Publication Data
McGuire, Barbara A.
  Creative Stamping in Polymer Clay / by Barbara McGuire
    p. cm.
  Includes index.
  ISBN 1-58180-155-6
  Polymer clay craft. 2. Rubber stamp printing. I. Title.
TT297 .M38697 2002
731.4'2—dc21
                    2001052207

EDITORS: Jane Friedman and Karen Roberts
DESIGNER: Andrea Short
PRODUCTION ARTIST: Cheryl VanDeMotter
PRODUCTION COORDINATOR: Sara Dumford
PHOTOGRAPHERS: Christine Polomsky and Al Parrish
PHOTO STYLIST: Laura Robinson

acknowledgements...

IT'S INCREDIBLE TO IMAGINE that somewhere in time someone experiences the same delight, the same discovery and still reaches toward a vision over and again. It may have been done before, but it is still new to me. I acknowledge the following persons and companies who have made vision a reality in my time.

MAGGIE, JANE, CHRISTINE AND GREG

POLYFORM

ARTISTIC WIRE

LIMITED EDITIONS

CAROL DUVALL

SUSAN MCNEIL

STEWART SUPERIOR

WELTER STENCIL

AMACO

ACCENT IMPORT

TIMESAVER TEMPLATES

NATIONAL POLYMER CLAY GUILD

* * *

The eye never has enough of seeing

Nor the ear its fill of hearing

What has been will be again

What has been done will be done again

There is nothing new under the sun.

* * *

dedication...

This book is dedicated to

Jean, Donna, Leigh, Pat, Alma, Jeannie, and Lisa

MY FOREVER FRIENDS.

INTRODUCTION

*

I WONDER WHAT DISTINGUISHES THE EXACT MOMENT OF CREATION FROM PREPA-

RATION, CONTEMPLATION, EXECUTION AND EVALUATION. I WONDER IF THE BLISS

OF CREATION IS PRESENT IN THE ENTIRE PROCESS, OR IF IT IS JUST PRESENT AT THE

MOMENT OF BIRTH. I WONDER WHAT DRIVES CREATION. **Is it curiosity? •**

Is it vanity? • Is it generosity? I WONDER ALL THESE THINGS

BECAUSE I CAN'T STOP CREATING.

The act of creating nourishes itself like an endless fountain drawing from its own well. Every so often, another spring feeds into the pool, refreshing the spirit and expanding the horizon. This is the goal of this book—to expand the horizon of those who love to create, to encourage those who love to discover. The everyday inventors of the twenty-first century are a life spring of ideas, colors, styles and expression. They have shared, shown and displayed the daydreams and imaginings conceived at kitchen tables, living room couches and airport terminals. It's because of a community of explorers that I have a book to present. The designs, the images, the colors, the illuminated finishes, the shimmering outlines are all available on demand because someone dared to make it happen.

When polymer clay arrived on the craft scene twenty to thirty years ago, several courageous and talented artists embraced it as their chosen medium. Since that time, interest in clay has blossomed and information has spread to the point where polymer clay will soon become an art essential. Simultaneously the amazing creativity emerging through the use of stamps is flourishing and is creating a social community of friends and developing artists with common interests and shared delight.

This book merges both interests into the vast potential of using stamped images with polymer clay. The projects are presented so that you will have a foundation on which to build and experiment, where even a slight variation, such as color, can create a completely new look or application. The techniques can apply to everything from jewelry to home decor items. Any of the suggested materials can be exchanged for your personal favorite powders, inks and designs. I have presented simple, classic designs, with focus on quality craftsmanship. The understatement of simplicity allows for appreciation of rich embellishments so you will enjoy adding your own meaningful touches that are so personal and dear.

Anything worth doing takes time. Skill requires practice. The great thing with clay and stamps is that it needn't always turn out the way it was intended. It can turn out better! And every alternative is not a mistake but a discovery that was meant to be. This book is a formal invitation to realize a vision and create something new under the sun. As Leonardo da Vinci said, "Lord, you give me everything for the price of an effort."

Anything worth doing takes time. Skill requires practice.

∗ ∗ ∗

polymer clay B A S I C S

POLYMER CLAY

Polymer clays are essentially plastic. All polymer clay is made with a combination of PVC, plasticizer, polyvinyl chloride and fillers. The plasticizer keeps the clay malleable until it is cured. When the clay is heated to a certain degree, the plasticizer is burned off in the baking. The types of plasticizer, PVC and fillers and their ratio determine the feel of the clay when raw and the strength of the clay when baked. This means that every brand of clay has unique properties because the formulas used in manufacturing are different. Some brand names include Fimo, Premo, Cernit and Sculpey. All of the clays are nontoxic, however, sensible precautions are recommended. Individuals who are sensitive to manmade materials should consult the Arts & Creative Institute (www.acminet.org) or the manufacturer for additional information. These instructions are not meant to be harsh—polymer clay is very user friendly—but intelligent precautions should be employed when using any art material, including powders, embossing materials and inks.

Use polymer clay in a designated place where it will not travel through a living area and possibly contaminate food areas. Anything that comes from the kitchen for use in polymer clay work should never be used for food thereafter.

WORK SURFACE

A nonporous work surface that cleans easily and is stain resistant should be used when working with polymer clay. Acrylic sheets, Formica, glass and marble are usually preferred. A small work surface is sometimes placed on top of a larger one in order to turn the piece being built or in order to move it to the oven without much handling. A measuring grid or a transparent surface over a grid is also helpful at times. The temperature of the work surface may also affect the clay. I do not personally prefer to work on marble because the stone draws the heat from the clay.

The ideal work surface is smooth and flat. The surface should be strong (does not mar easily) and remain securely in place when working on it. The surface should not react to the clay—certain plastics do and thus it might be wise to test a small area first. But it is somewhat advantageous if the clay adheres to a surface temporarily so the clay isn't sliding around. If the piece gets stuck, use a blade or knife to scrape under the clay and lift it from the surface. This may take a little practice.

You can use heavy cardstock as a disposable surface, but over time the surface will become marred with blade strokes and absorb plasticizer from the clay.

CONDITIONING

It is essential to condition all polymer clays. This aligns the molecules in the clay so that it is ready to respond to molding and forming. Conditioning increases clay strength and improves handling properties, stretching, texture and consistency. As you open the clay package, peel the wrapper back and cut off the desired amount. Don't cut through the cellophane, as little bits can get into your clay. Manipulate the clay, rolling it into a coil, folding and twisting it in your palms to make it pliable.

Repeat these motions until the clay moves easily in your hands. Brands will vary in character.

Some brands of clay may appear stiff until conditioned and others may be soft and squishy. Age and storage conditions will also affect the nature of the clay; over time clay becomes stiff. Light can also begin to age the clay, and since it is packaged in cellophane, direct sun can actually bake the clay in the wrapper.

If the clay is too stiff to roll into a coil, it can be warmed in your hands or tucked under a hot water bottle for five minutes. Using tools to help prepare the clay can eliminate discouragement and frustration when you are first working with it.

A small food processor is recommended if you are using stiff clay like Fimo Classic. Whirl small chunks of clay until the bits are warm to the touch—about one minute. The clay will begin to clump together when it is finished. It is possible to overdo this warming process, so be attentive. Clay is sensitive to friction and heat, which can begin to set the clay.

Condition by hand or slice a thin slab from the block and pass it through a pasta machine. Fold it onto itself and pass it through again. Repeat the process until the clay is pliable.

When you are mixing colors, you can mix at the same time you are conditioning. If you are using a processor, combine the colors as you chop the clay. If you are mixing by hand or with a pasta machine, you can combine bits or slabs of color to create new colors as you condition.

CONSISTENCY

To soften stiff clays, add mineral oil or dilutents or mix hard clay with softer clay. Brands can be mixed successfully, but I personally prefer to use the same brand consistently throughout a project to assure a consistent stretching and firmness. If you intend to use caning techniques in polymer clay, uniformity in clay consistency is critical.

To harden soft clays, leach out the plasticizer by placing flat sheets of clay on white paper. (Don't try this with inked paper; the ink will transfer to your clay.) The oily plasticizer will soak into the paper, making the clay stiffer. If you want to remove a lot of plasticizer, put weight on the paper/clay stack and change the papers as they become saturated. The surface of the clay touching the paper will "dry" and stiffen. It is necessary to reblend the clay to make it uniform.

STORAGE

Store clay in an airtight container, heavy freezer bag or waxed paper in a dark place. You can hold your unconditioned clays at the state they are in by freezing. A convenient way to store mixed colors is in a plastic organizer case. Some hard plastics such as acrylic will react to the clay. Never place raw clay on a computer or molded plastic equipment. Most likely it is made of PVC and the clay will adhere to it.

Thank You ... A few summers ago, seventeen professional authors, artists and teachers in the polymer clay community got together at Baby Island Lodge on Whidbey Island, Washington, and reviewed practices for working with polymer clay. The idea was to get everyone on the same page concerning terms frequently used in working with polymer clay. Discussions included how to prepare, cure and store clay, as well as how to use the equipment and what precautionary measures to take concerning toxicity. The following instructions draw greatly from those teachers' collaborative efforts, and I wish to credit those who contributed to the Polymer Clay Primer drafted at Whidbey Island, August 1999.

BA✴KING

Baking surfaces must withstand the heat of the oven. Cardstock, mat board or illustration board will not burn at 275°F (135°C). The surface should be flat and replaced if it becomes warped. Glass will also withstand baking temperatures, but clay that is baked directly on glass will have a shiny surface where the clay has rested on the glass. Glass or metal absorbs heat during baking and may not produce consistent temperatures throughout the piece.

Beads can be skewered on a suspended metal rod (or straight wire) to prevent any unwanted pressure on the bead form. The rods are suspended across a deep pan or polymer clay prop. Beads baked on a flat surface will have a slight flat spot. One solution is to bake beads upright, balanced on the hole, where the flat spot will be undetectable. Other props such as paper, cloth and polyester fiberfill can be made to accommodate baking items that are not flat.

Bake in an even heat source dedicated to your polymer clay work. For frequent use, a separate portable convection oven is preferable; a separate toaster oven is acceptable. Another alternative is to dedicate a large covered roasting pan to polymer clay if you bake in a home oven. This practice is recommended so that the plasticizer, which may collect on the inside of the oven, will collect on the interior of the roasting pan. This pan should never be used to contain food.

Temperature and length of baking is critical. Never assume that external knobs for "on" and "off" and temperature control are accurate. Always use an additional internal oven thermometer.

Do not allow the temperature to rise above what is recommended for the brand of clay you are using. Bake the clay according to the manufacturer's directions. Most clays are baked at 265–275°F (129°C–135°C) for 20 to 30 minutes. You can experiment by changing the length of time or lowering the temperature for translucent clays (to discourage browning), but never exceed 300°F (149°C). Burning polymer clay produces toxic fumes. Allow the clay to cool in the oven; or if the clay requires weighting or a rapid cooling, stand away from the oven as you open the door to avoid inhaling any fumes.

SAFETY

If accidental overbaking or burning of polymer clay happens, turn off the oven, open the windows and walk away. DO NOT open the oven door to let out the fumes. Let it cool until you can handle it with bare hands. DO NOT open a convection oven while in operation or you will get a blast of fumes. Safety equipment includes an oven mitt, oven timer and fire extinguisher. Convection ovens used heavily accumulate an oily residue on the oven walls and glass door. This should be periodically wiped out using paper towels and a lightweight glass cleaner.

To Preheat or Not to Preheat?

Some ovens can handle a cold start while some necessitate preheating. Most toaster ovens and some convection ovens have cycling thermostats that can be difficult to manage. Control rapid spikes in heat by preheating the oven to the proper temperature. Minimal opening and closing of the door also prevents heat loss and helps keep the heat steady so that the thermostat stays accurate. Never open an operating oven to just throw in one piece.

Large home ovens and some convection ovens (Farberware) have thermostats that gradually increase temperature and keep a reliable, steady heat. Work can be placed in the cold oven and brought up slowly to the correct temperature and held there. Intentional bumping up of temperature is achievable in these ovens. Bumping is a practice of raising the temperature slightly (to 300°F or 149°C) at the end of baking for a short period of time to assure all the clay has been completely cured. Bumping up a toaster oven is not recommended.

polymer clay TOOLS ✦ MATERIALS

Tools for working with polymer clay can be found everywhere, whether they are manufactured, a found object or homemade. A basic tool kit would include a tool to cut, a tool to roll, a tool to make holes and a tool to burnish.

PASTA MACHINE

A pasta machine is a good tool for conditioning clay. Designate the machine specifically to clay and do not use it again for food. The main difference in pasta machines is the settings and the width of the rollers. Some machines assign the widest setting at number one and other machines assign the widest setting at number seven. Most machines will have six to seven settings; the thinnest setting produces thinner sheets than you can achieve when rolling by hand. The machine usually comes with an attachment for cutting the clay into strips. You can also purchase a motor for the machines, which speeds the process and allows the use of both hands when conditioning and preparing clay. Wipe the machine with a paper towel after you change colors, as traces of clay can contaminate the next project or color. When conditioning, begin by setting the

rollers on the widest space. Stiff clay will need to be flattened with a rolling pin to about a $1/8$" (3 mm) thickness before it goes into the pasta machine. If the clay is a softer brand, such as Fimo Soft, Premo or Sculpey, you can slice thin slabs and put them directly into a pasta machine for conditioning. Make sure the slabs are thin enough not to jam the rollers. Run the clay through the rollers, reset the rollers to a thinner setting and roll again. The clay sheet can be folded and sent through at a double thickness. To minimize pockets or bubbles, always have the fold positioned to go through the roller first or turned vertically to the side.

ROLLING TOOLS

Rolling tools should have a smooth, even surface that the clay will not adhere to. It is also advantageous if they are clear. Clean the rolling tools often because they may pick up bits of clay or ink from a previous application. Some rolling tools I use are a solid Plexiglas rod, acrylic brayer, an even-sided glass or a wine bottle.

CUTTING TOOLS

Cutting tools are intended for dividing the clay into parts, creating edges, slicing and altering the surface of the clay and slicing canes. You must have an extremely sharp and straight blade to slice through the clay so it will not drag and distort the design in canes. Cutting tools are extremely dangerous; therefore, always take precautions when using a blade or knife. The application will dictate which blade you should use. Always protect the area or table being used for cutting. Make sure your fingers are out of the blade path.

The sharpest blades—tissue blades or polymer clay blades—are very thin and between 4" to 6" (10.2cm to 15.2cm) in length. They can be rigid or flexible and are often made from stainless steel. A blade should be replaced when it is dented, rusty or corroded.

Additional blades or cutting tools include X-acto or Excel knives, wallpaper blades (similar to tissue blades but not as thin), utility or nonserrated paring knives, rotary type cutters and ripple blades. The ripple blade is bent in waves and is used in the food industry. A razor blade is not preferred because the lip drags as it slices.

MAKING HOLES

When you are making beads, pendants and connecting parts of clay or objects, you may need to make holes. The tool should pierce the clay and not crack it apart. Use the tool with a drilling motion to lessen the stress of the intrusion. When you are nearly through the piece, switch directions and pierce the hole from the other side to make a smooth indentation rather than a protrusion at the beginning of the hole.

Needle tools for jewelry or ceramics are very straight and sharp. You may also use aluminum hat pins, tapestry needles and double-pointed knitting needles in an assortment of sizes.

BURNISHING TOOLS

Burnishing smoothes the surface of the clay, secures paper, gold leaf, transfer foils and cloth to the clay evenly and discourages air bubbles. Most artists prefer a bone folder that is a tool commonly used in bookmaking.

GLUE

Crafter's Pic Ultimate Tacky Glue or Sobo glue will work for almost all of your gluing needs, whether the clay is baked or not. Apply a thin coat and press the clay pieces together,

then bake as directed. You can also use glue to attach other items to clay (such as paper).

However, for bonding baked clay and metal jewelry findings, you'll need something strong. Use superglue, gel consistency, and apply as directed. Lightly sand the metal parts to assure adhesion. If the clay pieces are not properly baked, the clay will not adhere to the metal.

VARNISH

I often use matte or gloss varnishes made by the manufacturers of polymer clay, or you can try polyurethane gloss varnish. Apply thin coats with a soft brush and allow it to dry between coats. Don't feel as if every piece you make should be varnished; many artists prefer the matte finish of the clay itself, or the smooth gloss finish of buffed clay.

MISCELLANEOUS

Other materials that are useful to have on hand are heavy-duty plastic bags, plastic wrap or waxed paper, tracing paper or parchment paper, something to carry your work in, hand lotion, paper towels, a skin barrier cream or non-latex gloves.

which clay brand **SHOULD I USE?**

Clay should fit the artist's needs and intentions. The main characteristics that define the clay are the ease of conditioning (preparation); the strength of the clay when it is cured; and the flexibility of the clay before and after it is cured. A consideration when making canes is the ability of the clay to stretch and retain proportion during reduction. You may also consider color, texture, translucency and availability. Three clays manufactured by Polyform warrant special mention.

Premo metallic clay possesses a directional mica shift within the clay. This creates a holographic or ghost effect within the same color clay. Liquid Sculpey is a unique liquid polymer clay available in opaque and translucent form. Sculpey Flex is the only clay specifically designed to stretch and bend after baking.

The following is a basic description of the clay brands and their intended users.

SCULPEY

Sculpey, made by Polyform, is a soft clay, easily conditioned and widely available in a large variety of colors including glow-in-the-dark, metallic and pearl. It is popular with children and schools. Super Sculpey is a flesh-colored clay with translucent-like depth. It is very strong and popular with doll makers and sculptors. Premo Sculpey is clay formulated for artists and crafters. The color palette is based on oil color pigments and includes metallic and pearl clay with a mica shift. The clay has excellent durability and is easily conditioned. Sculpey Flex is available in primary colors and will retain flexibility after baking. Sculpey white is an original formulation of Polyform clay and continues to be a staple in the sculpting arts. Liquid Sculpey is the only liquid polymer clay. All Polyform products are manufactured in the United States.

CERNIT

Cernit, made by T&F Kunstoffe GmbH, is clay that is easily conditioned and is fairly strong. The glamour colors have a translucent quality that at times can resemble bakelite. Cernit is popular with doll makers because of the translucent quality in the doll clay. Cernit is manufactured in Germany.

FIMO

Fimo Soft, made by Eberhard Faber GmbH, is soft clay that is generally easy to condition but may vary in consistency due to different pigments or inclusions. The palette is based on trend colors and effect colors, which include dayglow, stone, metallic and translucent colors. Fimo Classic is firm clay that requires thorough conditioning. It is very strong and has a resilience that is popular in making canes. The classic colors are opaque with the exception of the translucent clay, which has a feature called plaguing. These are small pockets in the clay that create a stone-like effect. There are also doll clays in various shades available. Eberhard Faber GmbH manufactures modeling materials in Germany.

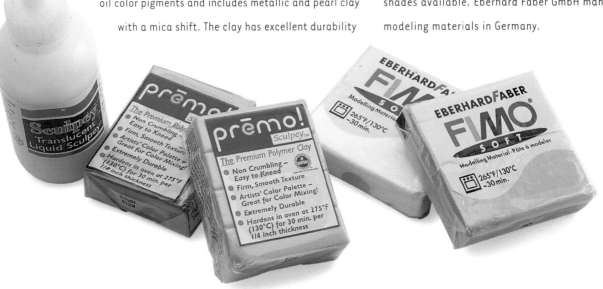

rubber stamps &MORE

RUBBER STAMPS

The stamps you may wish to consider when working with clay should be deeply cut. Stamps producing "line drawings" generally work very well.

You can make the negative version of a stamp by making a mold in polymer clay so that if you can't find a stamp with a negative relief, you can create your own mold to produce a raised image. See the instructions on page 21 for doing this.

I often remove the block of wood from the stamp. Thicker clay generally takes a better impression; or you can place a square of craft foam under thin sheets of clay to absorb the pressure of the stamp. The clay accepts the impression best when it has some give provided by sandwiching the clay between the stamp and the foam.

PIGMENT INKS

Often used to stamp directly on paper, pigment inks are your best choice for stamping directly on clay. The ink will set only when the clay is baked, so be careful not to smudge the ink while you're handling an uncured piece. I do not recommend dye-based inks as the ink will puddle on the surface of the clay.

POWDERED PIGMENTS (PEARLEX)

Powdered pigments are finely ground synthetic powders that can be applied to just about any surface, including polymer clay. Depending on the variety you use, the powder will add a metallic, iridescent or two-tone iridescent glow to your piece. You apply the powder to the clay with your finger or with a brush, and it bakes with the clay. Sometimes you may need to apply a sealant to the finished project to assure that the powder doesn't rub off over time.

GOLD LEAF

Imitation metallic, gold leaf (and other varieties, such as copper and silver) comes in extremely thin sheets that you can apply directly to polymer clay before or after baking. Because gold leaf will tarnish over time, be sure to use a sealant.

EMBOSSING POWDERS

Embossing powders can be successfully combined with polymer clay to create a variety of surface and imitative effects. It can be directly mixed into clay (try using translucent clay) and baked in the oven.

REFERENCE CHARTS

On the next few pages, you will find reference charts listing many of the materials you can use with polymer clay and polymer clay techniques. Many of the techniques are presented in the projects and others are reflected in the gallery. Please use this reference as an informative guide and as a suggestion for creative experimentation.

MATERIAL	DESCRIPTION	APPLICATION	CAUTION
> GOLD LEAF	thin sheet of composite metal stored between tissue paper; used to gild a surface; creates a crackle finish when stretched; used in mokume gane with translucent clay	apply directly to uncured clay; does not require adhesive; coat with varnish after baking to protect finish	gold leaf may tarnish and turn dark after many years, particularly in uncured clay
> PEARLESCENT PIGMENT POWDERS	synthetic powder finely ground, available in assorted colors; adds a metallic or iridescent glow to a surface	apply with finger or soft brush; bakes with clay but may require sealant for preservation	wearing a dust mask will prevent inhalation of fine powders
> INTERFERENCE PIGMENT POWDERS	synthetic powders finely ground that will shift color with the light; adds a two-tone iridescent effect on both white and black bases	apply with finger or soft brush; bakes with the clay; sealant may diminish effect; wipe off excess after baking	wearing a dust mask will prevent inhalation of fine powders
> PIGMENT INKS	ink used with embossing powders, opaque colors and metallics; defines stamped images	apply to stamp and press directly into clay; sets when baked; can be stamped on baked clay and cured in a second baking; can be removed with an eraser if on the surface or not stamped into the clay with pressure	test colors and opacity to ensure desired results and durability
> DYE-BASED INKS OR PERMANENT DYE INKS	ink designed for paper or porous surfaces; defines stamped images		dye-based inks are not recommended as the ink will puddle on the surface of the clay
> EMBOSSING POWDERS	traditionally used with pigment inks or embossing inks; endless varieties available; usually creates a raised surface	apply directly to uncured clay or mix into translucent clay for surface effects; bake with clay; achieve embossed effect with pigment or embossing inks in second baking	test materials if you want predictable results
> ACRYLIC PAINT	can be used as a wash to antique surfaces; adds color and depth	apply to cured clay; for minimal coverage, wipe with damp cloth; to antique, allow paint to dry, then sand lightly to remove top layer, leaving paint in crevices; wet sand with 400-, 600-, or 800-grit sandpaper; buff	take into account amount of paint and sanding and depth of impression to prevent loss of design

···art materials **REFERENCE**···

MATERIAL	DESCRIPTION	APPLICATION	CAUTION
> INCLUSIONS	glitter, mica flakes, sand, spices, fibers; creates effects with texture and color and often mimics stone	add mixtures to translucent clay	additive may rub off in exposed areas and stain; do not run coarse materials through a pasta machine
> LIQUID SCULPEY	liquid polymer clay, translucent and opaque; transfer medium and paintable medium; will bake clear on glass and creates flexible film of clay; acts as bonding agent between baked pieces (must cure in oven); clay softener	add powders or acrylic paint to color and paint with liquid clay; requires no finish	translucency depends on thickness of baked sheets; do not confuse translucent with opaque—both appear white before baking
> RELEASE AGENTS	cornstarch; use to prevent stamp from sticking to clay when impressed with water; use with Premo as a release	apply lightly and impress stamp	cornstarch will burn off in baking or can be wiped off
> PAPER	used as decoration or to add images and words; can be embedded or attached to polymer clay	apply with Sobo or Crafter's Pic Glue; can be varnished or embedded in a thin layer of translucent clay or Liquid Sculpey	
> METALLIC PIGMENTS	provides rich metallic coverage over surfaces and edges	apply directly to raw or baked clay; set by baking; permanent and requires no varnish	be sure to test colors; do not put solvent-based metallic rub-ons in the oven
> MARKERS	use gel pens on dark clays and permanent markers on light clays to create drawings or stamp impressions	apply directly to baked clay; color stamp and impress in raw clay; permanent finish	test for bleeding, color depth, and durability
> COLORED PENCILS	soft-lead, colored pencils or water soluble pencils; blendable; can be used for coloring transfers	color transfers before applying to clay; draw directly on baked clay; permanent after baking	
> CHALKS & PASTELS	deep artist's pastels and iridescent chalks for soft coloring	rub on clay before baking; bakes into the clay	

··· techniques **REFERENCE** ···

TECHNIQUE	DESCRIPTION
> MOKUME GANE	thin layers of stacked clay are distorted with an impression (such as from a rubber stamp), then slice or sand after baking to reveal variations; slices can be used for surface decoration, jewelry making and more
> MOKUME GANE (WITH GOLD LEAF)	layer sheets of gold leaf between ultra-thin layers of translucent clay; distort the stack and thinly slice horizontally through the layers; slices may be applied to many surfaces; sand, buff and polish finished pieces
> ANTIQUING	works well with textured pieces; paint finished pieces with raw umber or burnt sienna acrylic paint and then remove the paint on the top surface (with 400-, 600- and 800-grit wet sandpaper) while leaving it in crevices; buff to shine with a soft cloth; also used as a wash to shade smooth surfaces
> SKINNER BLEND	two or more colors of triangle sheets of clay are matched together to make a rectangle, then folded and passed through a pasta machine repeatedly, in the same direction, to create a graduation from one color to the next
> MICA SHIFT	use Premo Metallic clay; the mica in the clay, when aligned, reflects the light in a consistent direction; that reflection, when altered, creates a deeper color resulting in a holographic or ghost image (see the Ghost Pattern comb p. 82 for directions)

TECHNIQUE	DESCRIPTION
> TRANSFER — BLACK AND WHITE	place your image toner-side down onto the clay (ink-jet images don't work); allow image to set, then pull up paper—or remove paper after baking or soaking in water; do not touch until the item is cured during baking or toner will smear; can be covered with a thin layer of translucent clay; trapped air bubbles will not accept transfer; transfer time depends on clay, toner and temperature
> TRANSFER — COLOR	you can use ink jet transfer paper (t-shirt transfer paper) for color images; place image face down on the clay, bake and remove paper after item has cooled
> TEAR AWAY OR ETCHING	technique for etching the clay with a transfer image; the toner photocopy image sets on the clay just long enough for the toner to adhere, but when the paper is pulled up, it rips away clay; the etched clay is baked and rubbed with oil paint, which results in a look similar to scrimshaw
> CANING OR MILLEFIORI	a cane is a long rod of clay that has a design running all the way through that can only be seen on the ends; the cane is often reduced by stretching and rolling, then sliced with a very sharp blade; slices are used for jewelry or as surface decoration

making a **CLAY✳STAMP**

Here you will press a stamp into clay, resulting in a relief that is recessed. The relief is then baked and—presto—you have a new stamp useful for producing a raised image when pressed into clay. This play on texture produces interesting effects and is advantageous for the application of certain techniques.

MATERIALS LIST

- rubber stamp
- polymer clay
  (can be scrap pieces)
- cornstarch
- acrylic panel

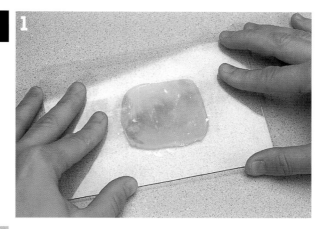

one

Condition the clay and roll it into a slab about ¹⁄₈" (3 mm) thick. You need it thick and large enough to accept the stamp. Coat the clay with cornstarch. Press the acrylic panel over the clay. This evens the texture and creates a truly flat plane.

two

Press the stamp into the clay with even pressure. Release the stamp and bake the mold.

three

Use the mold as a stamp to create a raised image in clay.

single stamp
ORNAMENT

There are countless images that when simply stamped into a sheet of clay can create a great ornament. Small details in finishing add refinement. The ornament will have more elegance with a beveled edge and a cleanly drilled hole. This same project will look classic stamped in metallic ink.

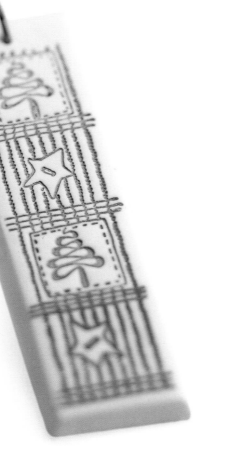

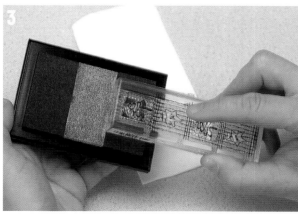

o n e

Condition the clay and prepare a slab about $^{3}/_{16}$"
(5mm) thick and large enough to stamp the image and
allow for a $^{1}/_{8}$" (3 mm) border.

t w o

Since the clay is white, it may pick up dust or small
pet hairs. Clean the surface of the clay by dragging a
blade gently over the top of the slab, removing the top
surface and clearing it completely of debris. Remove
the clay from the blade by pulling it off with a mound
of scrap clay. Don't remove it with your fingers.

t h r e e

Ink one portion of the stamp with a color of
pigment ink.

f o u r

Ink the remainder of the stamp in other colors. Do not
saturate the stamp. Only the lines of the image should
bear ink.

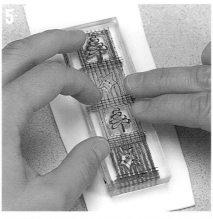

five

Press the stamp firmly into the clay and pull straight out. Since the clay will be baked, the pigment will bind to the clay. However, it will smear if you touch it before it is baked, so be very careful once you have impressed the stamp.

six

Bevel the edges of the design by cutting the clay with a tissue blade at a slant.

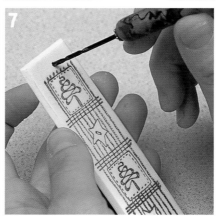

seven

Bake as the manufacturer directs. When the piece is cool, drill a hole through the top center of the ornament with a drill tool or a drill bit.

eight

Thread a length of cord (12" or 30cm) through the hole and tie into a bow. Slip the bow into the hole, creating a loop to hang the ornament.

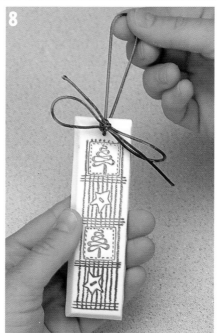

stamped
VOTIVE

This project can be colored any way you wish or even left sheer for a

delicate look. The light shines through the thinner clay, illuminating

the relief.

MATERIALS LIST

- glass votive
- white polymer clay
- deeply etched stamp
  (mine is a Stewart Superior
  Tattoo stamp)
- cornstarch
- polymer clay blade
- pink and gold PearlEx powder
- soft application brush
- damp cloth

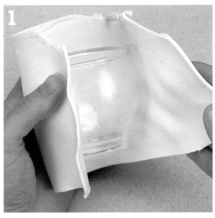

o n e

Prepare a thin layer of clay that will extend the cir-cumference and height of the votive. (Use a middle setting on a pasta machine; to achieve a ³⁄₃₂" or 2.5mm thickness). Cover the glass with the clay, stretching it slightly where the glass bulges. Release any air bubbles and smooth the clay to the glass. The clay will adhere to the slick sur-face of the glass.

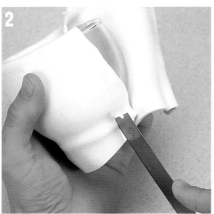

t w o

Score the clay with the blade vertically from top to bottom to make a straight edge.

t h r e e

Overlap the clay just enough to indicate where the clay joins and slice vertically to remove the excess clay.

f o u r

Smooth the seam with your fingers. You may need to dust your hands with cornstarch to help in handling the clay without fingerprints.

f i v e

Trim the bottom of the votive and tuck the top edge inside the votive. (It will be trimmed after it is imprinted).

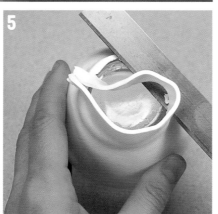

s i x

Dust the votive with a thin layer of cornstarch. Position a stamp to make a border around the top edge and press firmly. Stamp the next impression directly opposite the first. Slight over-lapping or variations are fine.

s e v e n

Trim the clay from the inside of the top using the glass edge as your guide.

e i g h t

Dust the clay with PearlEx. If the powder won't take due to excessive cornstarch, you can wipe the clay gently with a damp cloth.

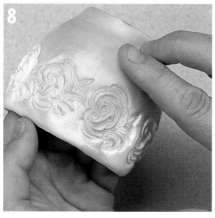

You can also use a brush to get in the deep relief.

n i n e

Overlay a layer of gold PearlEx powder to create a blown-glass finish. The powder will work into the polymer clay. Some powder may rub off after baking, but it will have a pearlescent shimmer. Bake as the manufacturer directs.

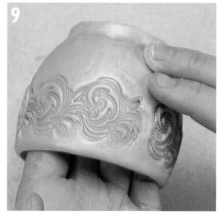

antique
PENDANT

This technique catches paint in the relief of the stamped design.

When the surface is wiped, the image is defined. It is an easy way to

make a striking piece. White, translucent or beige clay will each

present a slightly different look.

MATERIALS LIST

- translucent clay
  (this gives the clay a stone look)
- stamp (mine is Double Crane from Asian Images)
- acrylic paint
  (I'm using Liquitex Burnt Umber)
- deckle-edge scissors
- pendant cord
- cornstarch
- application brush or sponge
- damp cloth
- drill tool

ANTIQUING

Antiquing polymer clay was made popular by artist Tory Hughes, who is a master of imitating ivory, bone, stone and many organic and precious materials.

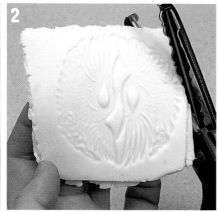

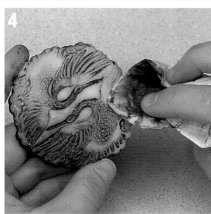

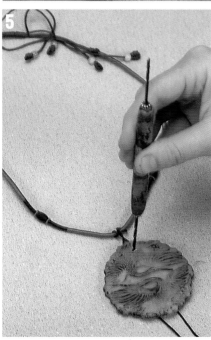

one

Condition the clay and prepare a sheet about ³/₁₆" (5mm) thick. Coat the clay with a thin layer of cornstarch to act as a release for the stamp. Impress the stamp into the clay.

two

Trim the edge with deckle-edge scissors. Bake the clay as the manufacturer directs.

three

When cool, paint the piece with acrylic paint. Be sure to get in the deep crevices and along the edges.

four

With a damp cloth, remove the paint as desired to highlight the relief.

five

Drill a hole and attach the pendant to the necklace.

big
BUTTON

Buttons can be decorative, but since you can wash polymer clay,

you can also make buttons for clothing. Test to make sure the clay

withstands the washing cycles and use heat-set inks. This button

shows a back made of plastic, but you can also design it with holes.

MATERIALS LIST

- **black polymer clay**
  (Fimo has proven very durable in
  washing for buttons)

- **paints or heat-set inks**
  (I'm using Dee's metallic inks
  by Ranger)

- **decorative-edge scissors**

- **Genesis varnish** (a heat-set
  paint medium) **or Liquid Sculpey**

- **glass surface for mixing colors**

- **stamp**
  (mine is from Art Seeds)

- **gold pigment inkpad**
  (I'm using Encore)

- **drill tool** (optional)

- **button back** (optional)

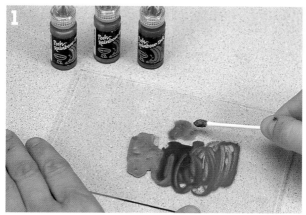

o n e

Squeeze a few colors of ink on a piece of glass.

t w o

Ink the stamp.

t h r e e

Prepare a slab of black clay ⅛" (3 mm) thick. Impress the stamp into the clay.

f o u r

Hold the gold inkpad and tap the top surface of the stamped relief.

five

Trim the design with a pair of decorative scissors. Bake the clay as the manufacturer directs.

six

Coat the clay with heat-set varnish. Bake the piece again for five minutes to set the varnish.

seven

Drill button holes or attach a button cover and attach to a pillow by slipping it over a sewn-on button.

little
BUTTONS

This is one of my favorite stamps, and it makes a great set of little

buttons. The powder is removed with fine sandpaper after baking.

This creates a contrast of black and gold and defines the design.

MATERIALS LIST

- black polymer clay
- rubber stamp
  (mine is from Magenta)
- PearlEx gold powder
- polymer clay blade
- button backs
- superglue
- 600-grit sandpaper

one

Condition and prepare a sheet of clay $1/8$" (3 mm) thick and large enough to impress the stamped design.

two

Coat the clay with gold powder.

three

Stamp the image firmly into the clay.

four

Using a polymer clay blade, split the design into squares. Bake as the manufacturer directs.

five

Face the button down and rub gently against wet sandpaper to remove the gold on the raised design. Do not sand too much or you will remove the design.

six

Glue the button backs on with superglue.

textured
BRACELET

Bangle bracelets are lots of fun to wear. Mix and match them for every occasion. The clay can be buffed to a shine that will make it look like polished stone.

 **FAUX JADE**

Jade colored clay is made by blending about one block of translucent clay with ¼" (6.5mm) diameter ball of green and ⅛" (3 mm) diameter ball of orange. The orange clay will dull the green. Vary the amounts to achieve the desired depth of color. You can also add bits of purple or even black clay, as well as green sand or green mica flakes.

MATERIALS LIST

- translucent polymer clay
- tiny bit of green and orange polymer clay
- brayer
- deep-relief stamp (mine is from American Art Stamp)
- cornstarch
- metallic bronze acrylic paint (for antiquing)
- 600-grit sandpaper
- polymer clay blade
- buffing pad or wheel (optional)
- ball end tool for smoothing (traditionally used for embossing designs in paper)

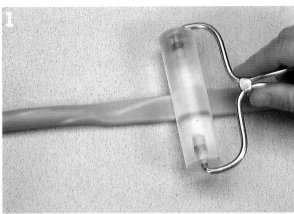

one

Roll a snake of faux jade clay about 1/2" (1.2 cm) in diameter and about 9" (22.8 cm) long. Flatten it evenly with a brayer to about 3/16" (5mm) thick.

two

Stretch the band at intervals and smooth it to make it even and consistent.

three

Rub it with cornstarch to serve as a release for the stamp.

four

Impress the stamp over the entire surface of the band.

(Note that I have pulled the stamp off its mounting block.)

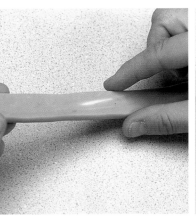

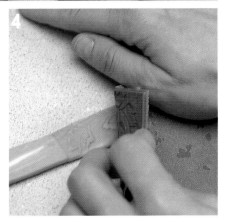

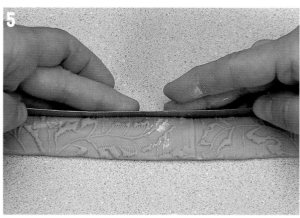

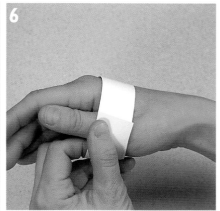

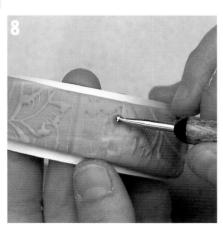

five

Use the flat side of a polymer clay blade to straighten the sides if uneven.

six

Cut a band of paper and measure your wrist at the widest point (usually at the bulk of the thumb).

seven

Tape the paper and use as a guide to measure the clay band. Cut the clay at an angle and press the seam together.

eight

Smooth the seams with a ball-end tool. Bake the clay as the manufacturer directs.

nine

Paint with acrylic paint and allow
to dry.

ten

Sand the raised surface of the design
with 600-grit wet sandpaper and water.

eleven

Polish the bracelet with a muslin
buffing pad for use with drills or a
jewelry buffing wheel.

disc
BEADS

These beads are simple and provide a flat surface for stamping.

The rolled clay is actually a cane and can be made more com-

plex by adding layers of different colors that will translate into

rings of color when sliced. This cane is known as a bull's-eye and

can be pinched into a triangle or flattened into a square for

versatile bead shapes.

MATERIALS LIST

- black and metallic yellow polymer clay
- polymer clay blade
- needle tool
- measuring tool (I'm using Mavx-it)
- silver pigment ink (I'm using Imprintz)
- collection of mini stamps (mine are from All Night Media)
- wire rod

o n e

Roll a snake of black clay ½" (1.3cm) in diameter. Rolling the clay under a piece of acrylic makes the snake even.

t w o

Prepare a sheet of metallic yellow clay ¹⁄₁₆" (1.5mm) thick and wrap it around the black snake.

t h r e e

Slice the overlap where the wrapped clay joins. If you slightly overwrap it, pull it back. The clay should have a faint impression that can serve as a guideline for slicing.

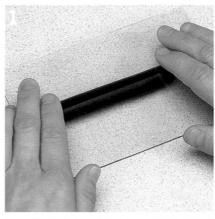

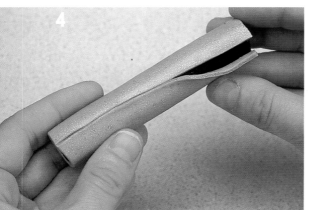

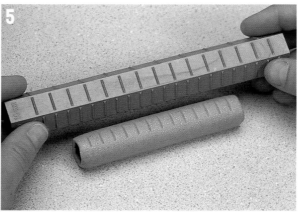

f o u r

Join and smooth the seams. Re-roll the snake to eliminate seams and, if needed, to reduce the cane. When you are making a lot of beads, work with a large diameter and reduce the cane (by rolling and stretching) to a smaller diameter.

f i v e

Mark equal amounts of the cane.

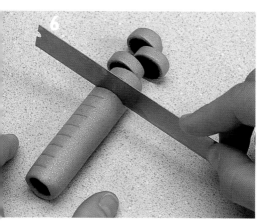

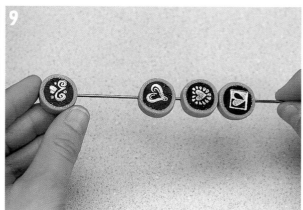

six

Slice through the cane with a back-and-forth rolling motion as the blade descends. This keeps the beads round.

seven

Stamp the beads with inked mini stamps.

eight

Pierce the beads with the needle tool. Rotate the bead and poke the hole through from the opposite side to make a smooth opening where the hole starts. Be mindful of the direction of the design and how it will string on the finished necklace.

nine

Place the beads on a rod for suspending during baking or the beads can lie flat. Just be careful of the ink because it still needs to heat-set. Bake the clay as the manufacturer directs.

wire
HEART PIN

Wire is a popular medium, and in this project, jump rings become

part of the embellishment. This decorative pin is created with a

unique stamp and is a perfect small gift. Use this project as an

inspiration for many other ideas using wire and other

embellishments.

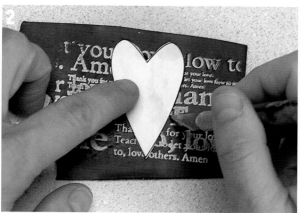

one

Condition and roll a thin sheet of navy blue clay and red clay (about $3/32$" or 2.5mm). Stamp the blue clay using gold pigment ink.

two

Carefully place the template on the clay and cut the design with the blade. Be careful not to smudge the ink as it is not yet heat-set. Set the piece aside.

three

Stamp the red clay with the same image using the gold ink.

four

Place the blue heart on the red stamped clay and cut a border about $7/32$" (5.5mm) wide.

five

Trim or straighten any edges with a flexible polymer clay blade as needed. Bake the piece according to the manufacturer's directions.

six

When the pieces are cool, drill small holes along one side of the inner heart.

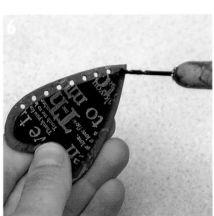

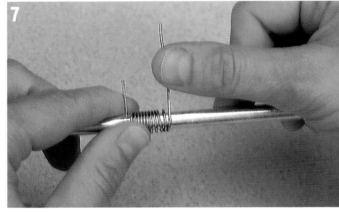

seven

Wrap the wire around the mandrel or metal tube. Remove the wrapped wire.

eight

Snip the metal rings apart using the flush cutters to separate the wire. This results in a beveled cut and a flush cut. The ring end should have a flush cut.

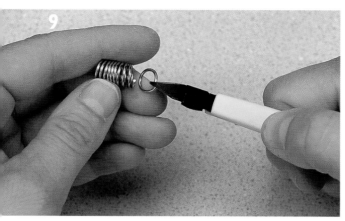

nine

Turn the pliers over to cut another ring so that the piece separating from the coil will have a flush cut on both ends. Then recut the coil and begin the process again, making a ring for each hole.

ten

Slip the rings through the hole and bend the wire back and forth to bring the ends together using the chain nose pliers and your fingers.

eleven

Cut a small rectangle of clay from the leftover blue scraps. Dab the back of the clay with a bit of glue and position it over the base of the pin back to secure it in place. Bake the piece again. This will secure the pin back without glue. Embedding the pin back before baking is the preferred method for attachment.

embossed
PENDANT

This lovely pendant features a stacked edge, and a clay bail accentuates the sleek line of the design. Using a negative stamp creates texture as well as an image. If your stamp will not produce a raised image, you can create your own clay stamp using the directions on page 21.

directions on page 21.

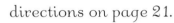

- metallic blue polymer clay and metallic red polymer clay mixed together in equal parts to create a deep purple

- one block of metallic silver polymer clay and $\frac{1}{8}$" (3 mm) block of metallic gold polymer lay mixed together to create a misty gray lime

- one block of black clay

- polymer clay blade

- Shapelets templates — classic design set (or create your own shape)

- tacky glue

- duo relief stamp (I'm using the Koi design from Creative Claystamp.)

- polymer clay varnish

- PearlEx pearlescent gold powder

- cornstarch

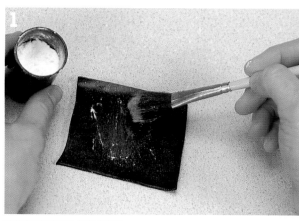

one

Prepare a thin sheet of clay (about $^3/_{32}$" or 2.5 mm) and coat it with cornstarch.

two

Press a sheet of purple clay into the mold side of the clay stamp. This will create an embossed design. You may have to dust your hands with corn-starch to keep them from sticking to the clay as you press.

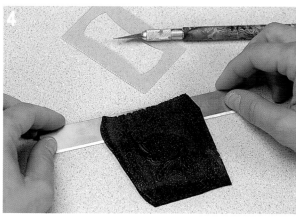

three

Position the template over the image and cut through the clay with a blade.

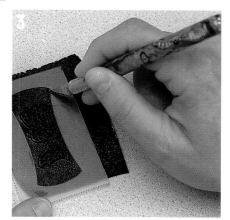

four

If the clay is stuck to the work sur-face, release the clay by sliding the polymer clay blade under the art.

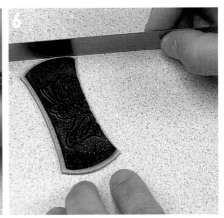

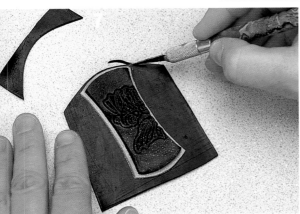

five

Place the cut piece on the green clay and begin to trim the shape, leaving a tiny edge alongside the original shape. This may take a little practice. Try pulling with your entire arm instead of bending your wrist.

six

Smooth and even the cuts by tapping the blade gently along the edge.

seven

Add another thin layer of contrasting clay.

eight

Lightly rub the raised surface of the design with pearlescent powder. Bake as the manufacturer directs.

nine

If you prefer a pin to a pendant, glue a pin back vertically with the clasp facing downward on the back of the piece.

··· to create a pendant ···

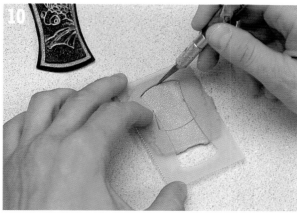

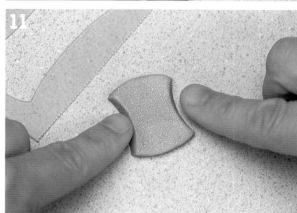

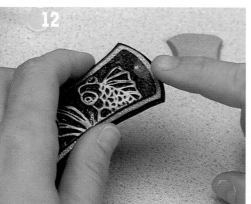

ten + eleven

Use the ends of the template as a guide to create a clay tab or bail to hang the pendant. This repeats the curves in the original design.

twelve

Place a small amount of glue on the baked pendant before you add the unbaked bail. This will ensure that the baked and unbaked clay will bond.

thirteen

Press the bail into place. Bake the piece again.

fourteen

When cool, coat with a layer of polymer clay varnish to pro-tect the pearlescent finish.

gold leaf
ACCORDION BOOK

Polymer clay is a great material to use as book covers. This book is

commonly called an accordion book and is filled with a strong

paper called mulberry paper. The fibers in the paper prevent the

pages from tearing.

MATERIALS LIST

- metallic gray and metallic blue polymer clay mixed in equal parts
- gold leaf
- mulberry paper
- bone folder
- leather cord
- beads or buttons
- tacky glue
- drill tool
- scissors
- 600-grit sandpaper
- tracing paper — cut to book size for pattern
- Celtic stamp
  (mine is from Nan Roche)
- polymer clay varnish

one

Condition and prepare two clay panels about ⅛"
(3 mm) thick. Use scissors to cut two sheets of gold
leaf. Holding the leaf between the tissue paper will
help to control the thin material.

two

Smooth the leaf on each sheet of clay; the gold leaf will
adhere to the raw clay without adhesive.

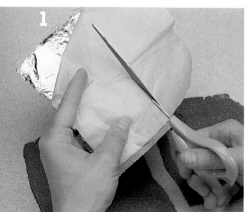

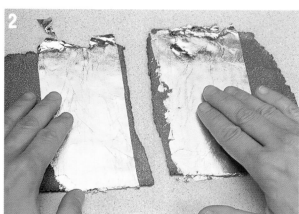

three

Center the design and stamp each sheet of clay.

four

Cut a piece of tracing paper to use as a pattern for
measuring the size of the book. Using the pattern,
center the stamp and cut both the front and back
panels of the book. Bake the clay panels as the manufacturer directs. If the panels have warped during
baking, weigh them down with heavy books during the
cooling process; this will flatten the panels.

five

When the panels are completely cool, use a damp sheet of 600-grit wet sandpaper to remove the gold from the top surface of the book panel. The gold leaf will remain in the recessed stamped design.

six

Prepare the inside pages by cutting a strip of mulberry paper at least as tall and eight times as wide as the tracing paper pattern. Measure slightly shorter for the width to allow for a slight variance in the folds. Fold the pages back and forth accordion style.

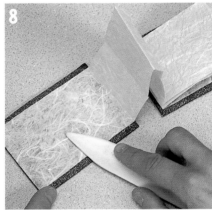

seven

Once the paper is folded, trim it to $^7/_{32}$" (5.5mm) less than the height of the book.

eight

Center one end of the paper on the inside of the front book panel and adhere with glue. Use the bone folder to smooth and secure the paper.

nine

Attach the back panel to the paper in the same manner.

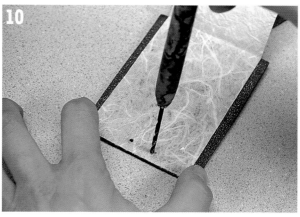

ten

Drill two holes centered on each side of each book panel.

eleven

Place the front and back panels alongside each other to measure the distance for drilling.

twelve

On the front book panel, thread a leather cord through the holes, slip a button through the cord and knot. The button should be loose enough to extend to the edge of the book.

thirteen

On the back book panel, make a cord loop on the outside of the panel and secure with a knot on the inside of the panel. The loop should be loose enough to fit over the button on the front panel when the book is closed.

fourteen

Varnish the stamped design to protect the leaf.

wooden
TASSEL COVER

You can decorate just about anything with a stamped piece of clay.

The secret is to cover the items first with a thin layer of tacky glue.

This helps bond the clay to the surface of wood, paper, cloth or

even baked polymer clay. Be sure the item you are covering

can withstand oven temperatures required for curing

the clay. **NOTE: DO NOT BAKE PAINTED, VARNISHED OR PLASTIC ITEMS.

MATERIALS LIST

- white polymer clay
- wooden eggcup
- saw
- ¼" (6.5mm) drill
- tassel to fill eggcup
- tacky glue
- brush and/or sponge
- gold heat-set paint
- stamp
  (mine is from Judikins)
- cornstarch
- polymer clay blade

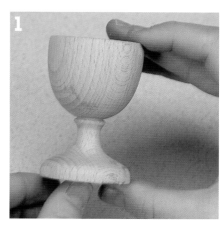

one + two

Saw the stem apart from the cup and drill a hole through the bottom of the cup.

three

Coat the cup with glue and set aside to dry.

four

Condition and flatten a strip of clay long and wide enough to cover the entire cup. Dust the clay with cornstarch and stamp the image into the clay.

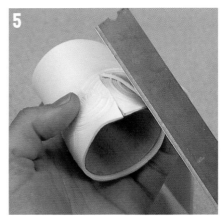

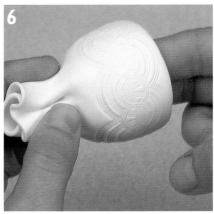

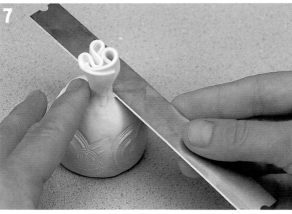

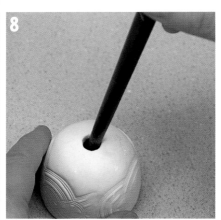

f i v e

Wrap the clay around the cup. Where the clay overlaps, cut the clay vertically, discard the excess and smooth the two edges together.

s i x

Pinch, pull gently and stretch the clay to smooth over the curve of the cup.

s e v e n

Slice the excess clay from the top of the cup.

e i g h t

Use the tip of a brush to smooth the hole.

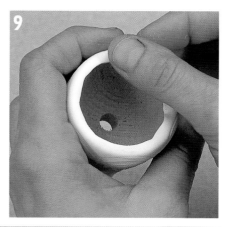

nine

Tuck and smooth the bottom edge of the clay into the inside of the cup. Bake the cup according to the clay manufacturer's directions. Allow to cool.

ten

Highlight the relief by applying gold heat-set paint. Use your finger or a dense sponge so the paint is only applied to the raised surface areas. Rebake the piece for two minutes to set the paint.

eleven

Pull the tassel cord through the cup to attach the cup to the tassel.

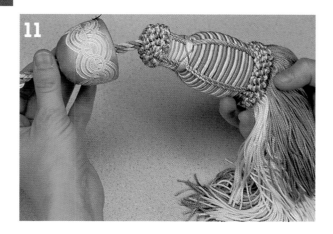

THE NEXT SERIES OF PROJECTS incorporates a technique called mokume gane. It is a Japanese metal layering technique where thin layers are stacked and altered or distorted. Subsequent slices through the layers reveal colors and patterns that have emerged through the altering process. Stamping into clay alters the layers and, when sliced, reveals the design of the stamp. This technique is spontaneous and delightfully unpredictable. The secret is to choose compatible colors of high contrast and make the layers as thin as possible. Practice will give you a control that yields numerous projects from one stack of clay.

Many artists working in polymer clay have discovered and experimented with unique ways to stack, slice and distort the layers of mokume gane. In particular, Tory Hughes, Lindley Huanani, Nan Roche and Celie Fago have inspired and influenced me with their incredible work, and I wish to acknowledge them. When you are choosing a rubber stamp for these projects, choose a design that has deep impressions and clear lines. Shallow-imaged stamps will not create enough variation in the distortion of the layers. Stamps that produce a negative image or raise the texture of the design work extremely well. Refer to page 21 for instructions on making a mold or negative stamp image that will work well with mokume gane.

mokume gane
NEEDLE CASE

You can cover any object you like with mokume gane—here I'm using a small and simple needle case. Feel free to use whatever is lying around, including your own clay tools. You'll soon find how exciting it is to experiment with this beautiful technique.

MATERIALS LIST

- metallic silver polymer clay (one block) and yellow polymer clay (¹/₈ (3 mm) block) mixed to make pastel lime clay

- metallic blue and metallic red polymer clay mixed in equal parts to make purple clay

- polymer clay blade

- rubber stamps (mine are from Hanko Designs)

- cornstarch

- wooden needle case

- tacky glue

- roller

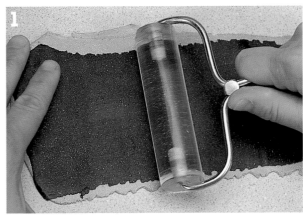

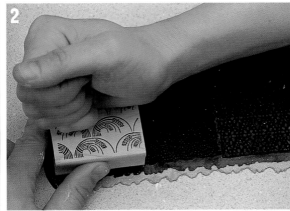

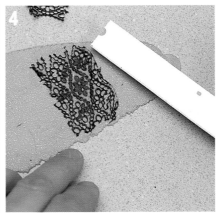

one

Begin by rolling a sheet of pastel lime clay (mix color as directed on page 59) to about $3/32$" (2.5mm) thick. Prepare another sheet of green clay to "catch" the pieces sliced in the process. Set the second sheet aside. Prepare a sheet of purple clay as thin as possible, about $1/64$" (less than half a millimeter). Stack the purple layer on top of one of the lime sheets and smooth with roller.

two

Dust with cornstarch and impress the stamp into the clay. A deep impression is crucial.

three

Use the flexible blade to slice an extremely thin layer from the stacked clay. The design in the stamp will emerge as the top layer is removed.

four

Place the removed slices on the sheet of lime clay set aside to "catch" the slices. This is not scrap and will later be used to cover beads. Set aside.

five

Coat the wooden needle case with glue. Allow to dry.

six

From your mokume gane stack, cut a rectangle of clay wide and long enough to wrap the needle case. Release any air pockets by making a small slice sideways into the pocket and smoothing the clay into place as the air is released.

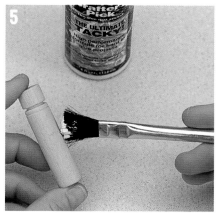

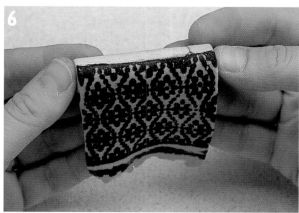

seven

Slice vertically where the clay overlaps and carefully smooth the seam.

eight

Slice the indent where the cap meets the body of the needle case.

n i n e
Remove the excess from the top and bottom of the needle case.

t e n
Place the top and bottom of the case on the lime clay and cut along the edge.

e l e v e n
Smooth the seams along the top and bottom edges. Bake the whole piece according to the manufacturer's directions.

mokume
BEADS

These gorgeous beads are actually made from the leftovers of the last project! All you need in order to make these beads are an acrylic disk and a needle tool. Clay artist Tory Hughes introduced this cone shape, and it has a thousand variations. You can experiment and use your imagination to create your own variation.

one

Use scrap clay to make a ball about 1" (2.5cm) in diameter.

two

Cover the ball with the patterned clay that was set aside from the mokume gane needle case project.

three

Pinch or twist the ends and slice away the excess.

four

Place the bead under the acrylic disk. Bear down and roll the disk in a circular motion until the bead results in a cone shape. Varying the pressure and angle of the disk will produce different cone shapes.

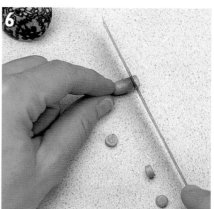

five

Poke a hole through both points of the cone using the needle tool. Handle the bead lightly. Remember to reverse the bead and poke through from both ends to make a smooth hole.

six

Roll a small snake of lime green clay and slice small disks.

seven

Place a disk over the hole of the bead. This puts a little cap at the top of the bead and adds a finishing touch.

eight

Poke a hole through the cap and bake the bead according to manufacturer's directions suspended on a metal rod.

covered
TOOLS

You may have noticed that throughout the book the tools I have used are often covered with clay. These tools were created using bits and pieces from other projects. This creates an interesting surface design that will enhance your tools. Artist Celie Fago introduced this concept that reflects individual taste and style.

... covered burnisher

- polymer clay leftovers from the Mokume Gane Needle Case project or create a sheet of mokume gane specifically to cover your tools (follow the technique instructions starting on page 60)

- your choice of tools to cover in clay (except for plastic tools)

- tacky glue

- metal rod

- polymer clay blade

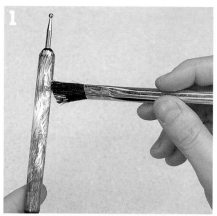

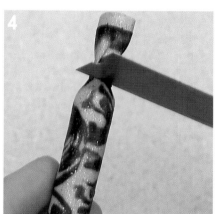

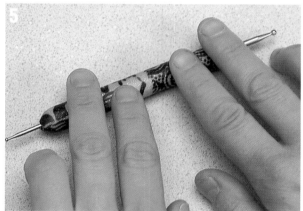

one

Coat the wood handle of your tool with glue and allow to dry.

two

Cut a straight edge on the prepared sheet of clay and wrap around the tool.

three

Slice and remove the overlapping clay. Smooth any air pockets.

four

Pinch and slice away the excess clay at the end of the handle.

five

Roll the surface to make the handle smooth.

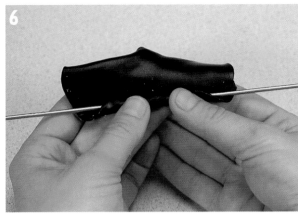

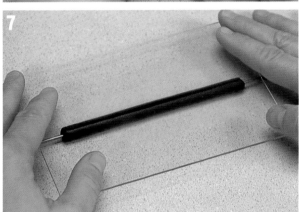

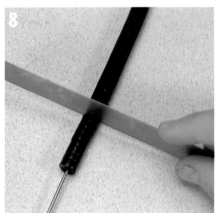

six + seven

Wrap a metal rod with a thin sheet of purple clay until it has a ¼" (6.5mm) diameter. Roll it into a smooth cylinder.

eight

Slice small disks about ⅛"(3 mm) thick.

nine

Poke a hole through the disks and secure them as caps to the handle of the tool. Bake as the manufacturer directs.

Depending on your design, you may want to embellish the clay with PearlEx powder.

mokume gane
CYLINDER BEAD

Mokume gane can be made of as many layers as you wish. The
challenge is to choose colors that have a high contrast but do not
clash. Using white and black will help to achieve success in color
harmony if you are uncertain of your choices.

MATERIALS LIST

- yellow, turquoise, brown and
  salmon (a mixed color of beige
  and a tiny bit of red) polymer
  clay — conditioned and rolled
  into as very thin sheets

- extremely thin sheet of
  translucent polymer clay to
  "catch" slices

- thin sheet of white
  polymer clay

- polymer clay blade

- roller

- pasta machine

- cornstarch

- bone disk beads, ½" (1.3cm)
  diameter with a large hole
  (you'll need two disks for each
  clay bead)

- set of themed stamps
  (I'm using Egyptian Creative Clay
  stamps, and both the positive and
  negative side of the stamps helped
  create the images in the clay)

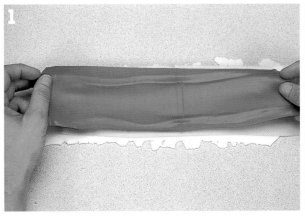

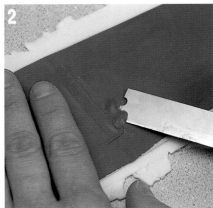

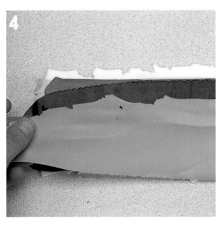

one

Condition and mix the colors. Roll the colored clay into thin sheets. Make one base sheet of translucent clay (1/32" or 1mm). Stretch an ultrathin layer of yellow clay, then turquoise clay on top.

two

The layer should be as thin as possible and there should be no air bubbles. If a pocket of air occurs between the layers, slice the bubble from the side using the blade. Slicing from the side will discreetly mend the opening.

three

Smooth the clay back together, releasing the air.

four

Continue to stack layers in the following sequence: yellow, turquoise, brown, salmon. Once the clay is stacked, flatten it even more to thin out the layers.

(Use the pasta machine or a roller.)

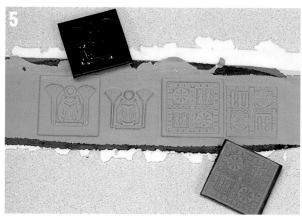

five

Dust the layers with cornstarch and impress the stamps using both the positive and negative relief. If you are using Polyform clay, you can use water as a release.

six

Carefully slice through the top layer with a polymer clay blade.

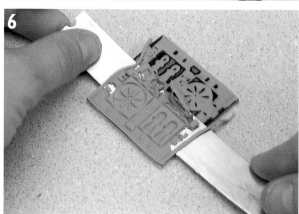

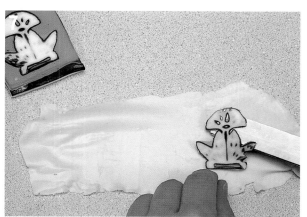

seven

Place the sliced pieces on a thin sheet of white clay. This will be used in another project (see Bits and Pieces Bracelet p. 76). If the slices will not stick you can remove the cornstarch from the impressed stack with a damp cloth after the image is impressed and the stamp is released.

eight

Slice through the layers until you have colors and revealed designs of your liking. The thinner you cut the layers the more colors will be revealed.

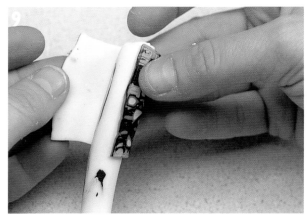

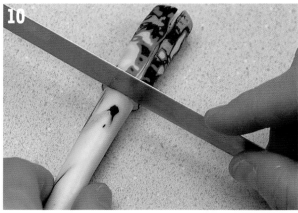

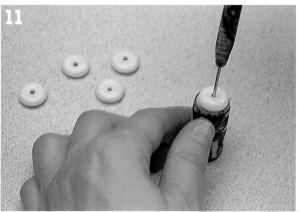

nine

Roll a cylinder of translucent clay about 1/2" (1.3cm) in diameter. Cut the stamped and sliced designs in square sheets to fit around the cylinder.

ten

Smooth the seams and trim the ends.

eleven

Make a hole with a needle tool extending through the bead. Place a bone disk bead on each end of the cylinder. Bake the clay as the manufacturer directs.

mokume gane
SCRAP PIN

Many times you will have small scrap strips that can still be utilized.

Line them up next to each other and you have a new sheet of

mokume gane to stamp.

YOU'LL NEED THE SAME MATERIALS USED FOR THE CYLINDER BEAD PROJECT (P. 69) PLUS THE FOLLOWING:

- negative relief stamp
  (I'm using the Nile Flower from Creative Claystamp)

- turquoise pigment ink

- translucent polymer clay
  in a prepared sheet
  1/8" (3 mm) thick

- pin back

- superglue

- tacky glue

- roller

MATERIALS LIST

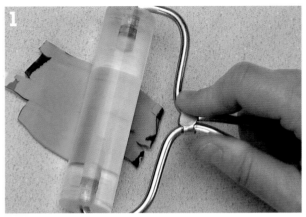

one

Align your scraps next to each other and thin them out with a roller.

two

Dust the clay with cornstarch and use a negative relief stamp to raise the image.

three

Slice the top layer to reveal the color and design. Cut with the flexible blade to create an arched and angled border. Bake the clay as the manufacturer directs.

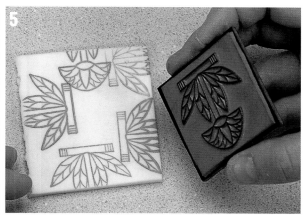

four

To make the translucent border, start by inking the positive side of a stamp with pigment ink.

five

Press portions of the inked image into a sheet of translucent clay.

six

Press the baked clay into the unbaked translucent clay. Add a dab of tacky glue to the back of the baked piece to assure bonding.

seven

Trim the edges. Bake the piece again. Attach a pin back with superglue.

bits and pieces
BRACELET

This great bangle not only makes use of scraps, but also creates a veiled or subtle frosted look. The colored bits are embedded in a thin layer of translucent clay, which when baked, clears enough to give depth to the finished piece.

MATERIALS LIST

• translucent and white polymer clay

• remnant pieces from a mokume gane project

• gold PearlEx powder

one: PREPARATION

Condition and roll out a thin sheet of white clay about 2" x 8" (5cm x 20cm). This strip will become the outer decoration for the bracelet. From a mokume gane stack or previous project (such as the Mokume Gane Cylinder Bead p. 69), place some bits and pieces on the white clay strip.

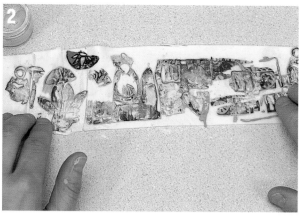

two

Use your finger to apply a bit of PearlEx powder, and press the slices firmly into the sheet. Do not apply excessive amounts of powder.

three

Roll a long strip of translucent clay on the thinnest setting of the pasta machine. If the thinnest setting is not manageable, use a thicker setting and stretch the clay. Place it over the prepared strip.

four

Press the clay together securely; you can make small patches with translucent clay if necessary. The goal is to get a very thin layer of translucent clay over your prepared strip.

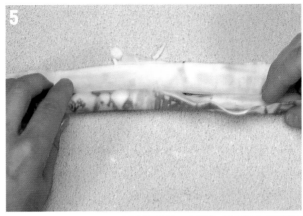

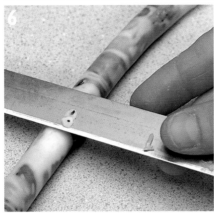

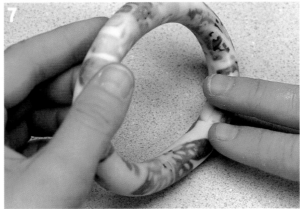

five

Roll a snake of white clay about 8" (20cm) long and
³/₈" (1cm) wide. You can also use scrap clay, as it will
be hidden inside the bracelet. Cover the snake with the
prepared strip (this will increase the diameter).

six

Roll the band on a hard surface to smooth the seams
and remove any debris from the surface of the band.

seven

Measure the length needed for the size of the bracelet
(see the Textured Bracelet project p. 35 for instructions). Blunt
cut the ends, and press the two ends together. Stand
the bracelet upright and gently roll on a hard surface
to smooth the joint. Bake as the manufacturer directs.

Note: This bracelet looks awesome when it is polished. The
translucent clay resembles glass.

big
EMBOSSED BEAD

Here's another way to use scrap clay and interesting shavings from a mokume gane stack. The silver bead caps add an exquisite finishing touch. Just be aware that the bead cap holes need to be large enough for the intended string.

MATERIALS LIST

- translucent and white polymer clay
- scrap clay
- mokume gane shavings
- needle tool
- two Bali silver bead caps
- 400-, 600- and 800-grit sandpaper
- metal rod
- buffing wheel

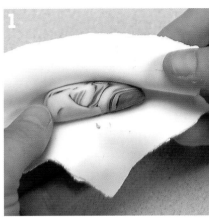

one

Roll a blimp-shaped bead from scrap clay. Cover the bead with white clay.

two

Roll the bead until it is smooth.

three

Place the mokume gane shavings on an extremely thin sheet of translucent clay.

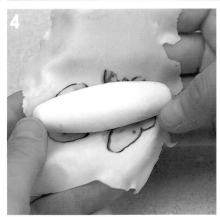

four

Cover the white bead with the translucent-embedded design. The translucent clay should be on the outside of the bead, and the design should be showing through the translucent clay.

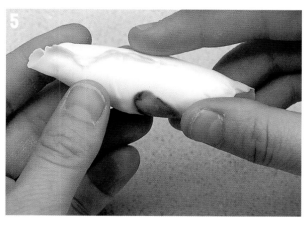

five

Overlap and smooth the seams. The bead may start to take a different shape similar to a cigar.

six

Pierce a hole through each end with a needle tool.

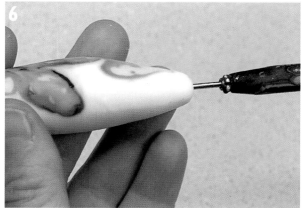

seven

Place the bead caps on each end and bake on a metal rod according to manufacturer's instructions. Note: This bead will look wonderful if polished. Wet 400-, 600- and 800-grit sandpaper and polish on a buffing wheel.

ghost PATTERN COMB

The following project illustrates one of the most fascinating features of mica shift clay. Little particles in the clay reflect the light at different angles, giving depth and illumination to the design pressed into the clay. This particular technique is similar to mokume gane, but there are no layers. Here I've chosen to cover a comb, but choose whatever item suits your fancy.

MATERIALS LIST

- wooden comb
- tacky glue
- application brush
- Premo Metallic Gold polymer clay
- craft knife
- deep impression rubber stamp (mine is Kimono by Limited Editions)
- acrylic brayer
- polymer clay blade

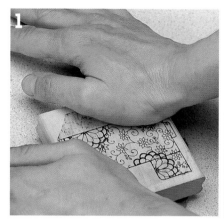
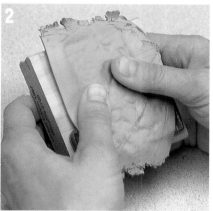
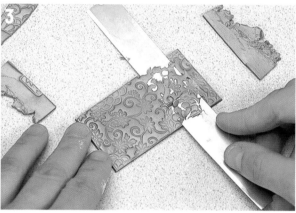
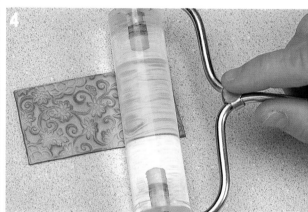

one

Condition and prepare a sheet of gold clay approximately $1/8$" (3 mm) thick. Make sure it is well conditioned because this is what will cause the little mica pieces to align. Fold the sheet in the same direction each time you pass it through the pasta machine. Dampen the sheet with water and press the stamp firmly into the clay.

two

Flip the sheet without removing the stamp, and press the clay into the stamp with your fingers to achieve a deep impression.

three

Trim to the approximate size needed to cover the comb. Slice a very thin top layer from the impressed clay. The surface will be smooth and the design will be revealed in the shifting mica.

four

Lightly roll with a brayer to smooth the surface.

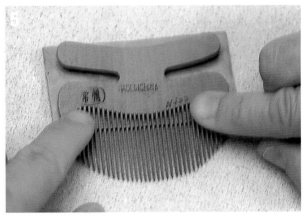

five

Place the design face down and position the comb on the back of the sheet.

six

Lightly press the comb into the clay just enough to make an impression of the teeth in the comb. The definition will be your guide for cutting.

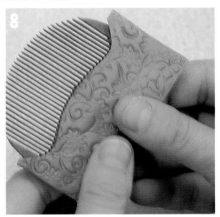

seven

Coat the comb with the glue in the areas to be covered with clay. Allow to dry.

eight

Attach the trimmed piece to the comb, being careful not to trap any air bubbles.

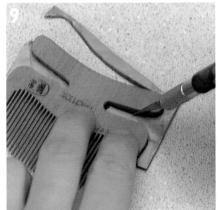

nine

Trim the excess clay. Cover the backside in the same manner. You may wish to use another color of metallic mica clay. Bake as the manufacturer directs. Wood will withstand low baking temperatures. Varnish or sanding will bring out more depth in the design.

clay painted
BUTTERFLY

The special clay used in this project is in liquid form. It can be used as a paint to color the surface, to marble, and to transfer copier images. Using an image that produces raised lines, the liquid polymer easily falls within the grooves and creates a faux cloisonné effect.

MATERIALS LIST

- Liquid Sculpey
- PearlEx powder
- butterfly stamp (mine is from Delta)
- Premo metallic gold polymer clay
- craft knife
- application brush
- pin back
- superglue
- piece of glass

o n e

Make a mold or "clay stamp" from the butterfly stamp. See instructions on page 21.

t w o

Roll a thin sheet of gold clay about $\frac{1}{3}$"(3 mm) thick. Dampen with water. Use the molded piece to impress into the gold clay.

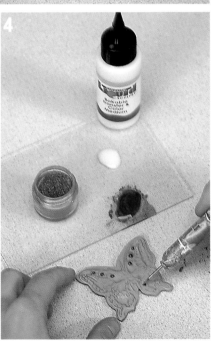

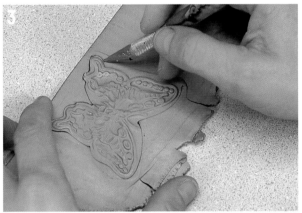

t h r e e

Cut out the outline of the butterfly and bake the clay as the manufacturer directs.

f o u r

Mix a tiny amount of the PearlEx powder to the liquid clay. Use a piece of glass to act as a mixing palette. Apply the paint to the baked butterfly, filling in complete areas or using dots of color. Bake the butterfly again. Attach a pin back with superglue to make a lovely brooch.

textured
COLLAGE FRAME

You can turn any frame into a beautiful textured collage using

your favorite stamps. This frame uses PearlEx powder as the

release agent. The project also shows how to turn an image into a

stamp by tracing and carving a rubber block.

MATERIALS LIST

- wooden frame
- polymer clay
- tacky glue
- craft knife or polymer clay blade
- bone folder or burnishing tool
- PearlEx powder
- application brush
- variety of stamps
- white acrylic paint
- decorative parchment paper
- outlined butterflies
  (stamped and baked or premade)

IF YOU MAKE THE OUTLINED BUTTERFLIES, YOU'LL NEED:

Rubber carving block • Speedball carving tool with tiny nib • Tracing paper • Pencil • Craft knife • Printed image • White clay • PearlEx powder

o n e

Cover the wooden frame with glue. The glue will provide a tacky surface to adhere the clay.

t w o

When the glue is dry, place a thin sheet of polymer clay approximately $\frac{1}{8}$" (3 mm) thick on the frame. Trim the excess clay.

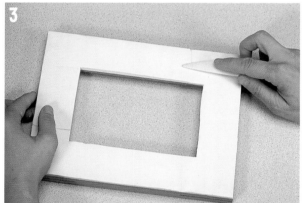

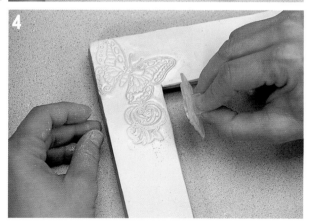

t h r e e

Smooth the seams with a bone folder or burnisher.

f o u r

Dust the stamps with PearlEx powder and press firmly into the clay in a random design.

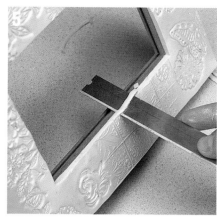

five

Again trim any clay that may extend over the frame. Bake as the manufacturer directs. The wood frame will withstand low oven temperatures.

six

When the frame is cool, paint the edges of the frame.

seven

Cover the photo panel with parchment. Glue the butterflies to the parchment.

eight

Insert the panel into the frame.

··· how to make **outlined butterflies** ···

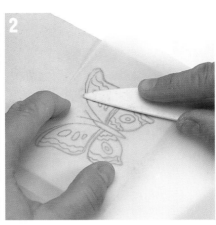

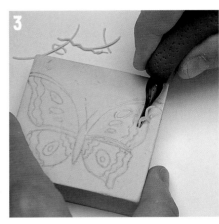

one

Using your background image as a guide, trace and outline a butterfly in pencil. Add unique variations to your design as desired.

two

Place the tracing paper graphite side down and burnish the design onto the rubber block.

three

Carve the transferred lines with the carving tool.

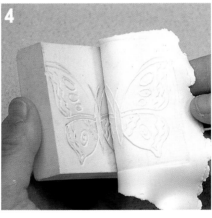

four

Impress a sheet of white clay to create the butterfly.

five

Trim the butterfly with a craft knife.

six

Dust the butterfly with PearlEx powder. Bake clay as the manufacturer directs.

chunky
COLLAGE BRACELET

The design in this bracelet runs completely around the wrist but is sectioned so the bracelet can bend. The pieces are angled to accommodate the curve of the band.

MATERIALS LIST

- white and champagne polymer clay
- polymer clay blade
- set of stamps
  (mine are from the Nick Bantok collection by Limited Editions)
- gold and black pigment ink
- drill
- elastic cord
- paper, tape and scissors
- pasta machine

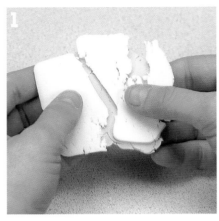

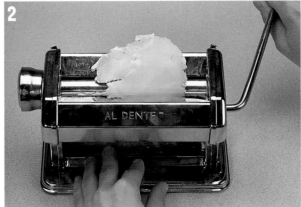

one

Combine thin sheets of two conditioned clay colors.

two

Press the colors together through the pasta machine.

three

Stop when the clay is sufficiently marbled. Do not completely blend the color.

four

Make a band to fit your wrist with paper and tape.

f i v e

Cut the band apart.

s i x

Roll an even strip of clay ¹/₄"
(6.5mm) thick, 1¹/₂" (3.8cm)
wide, and trim it to the length
of the band.

s e v e n

Decorate the clay strip with a
collage of images using black
and gold inks. Be careful not
to smear the ink. It will be wet
until it is baked.

e i g h t

Cut the strip into sections 1"
(2.5cm) wide, or whatever
length will accommodate
equal pieces to fit within the
length of the bracelet.

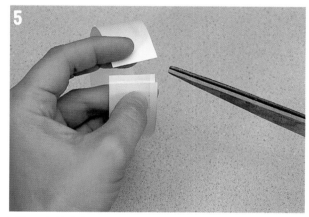

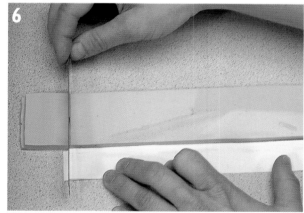

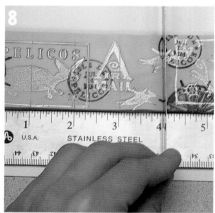

nine

Use the side of the blade to straighten and smooth the top and bottom edges.

ten

Bake the clay as manufacturer directs. Drill holes horizontally through the sections near the top and bottom where the cord will be inserted.

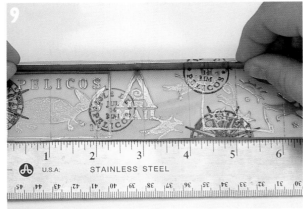

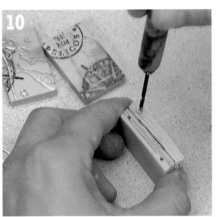

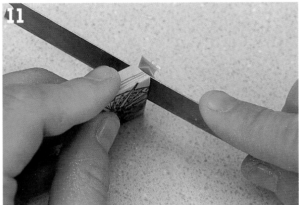

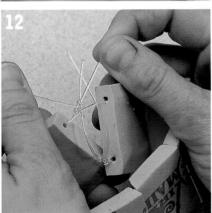

eleven

Slice the edges, angling inward to accommodate the turn in the bracelet.

twelve

Thread elastic cord through the holes and secure with a knot.

veneered
IMPORT BASKET

You can put polymer clay on just about anything and enhance simple

pieces with your design. Import stores are a great place to find baskets

and boxes just waiting for a personal touch. These panels are actually

a veneer applied after they have been baked.

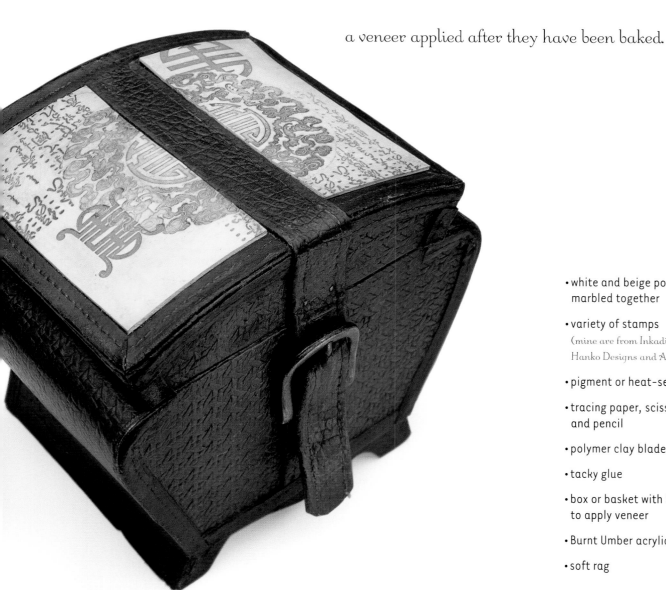

- white and beige polymer clay
  marbled together

- variety of stamps
  (mine are from Inkadinkadoo,
  Hanko Designs and Asian Images)

- pigment or heat-set inks

- tracing paper, scissors
  and pencil

- polymer clay blade

- tacky glue

- box or basket with inset area
  to apply veneer

- Burnt Umber acrylic paint

- soft rag

one

Roll a thin sheet ($1/32$" to $1/16$" or about a millimeter) of clay to fit in the chosen box or basket inset area and ink a stamp.

two

Imprint the design onto the clay.

three

Continue to create a collage. Use contrasting colors to highlight.

four

Mask areas you do not want to overlay images with tracing paper.

five

Add interest using a variety of image sizes.

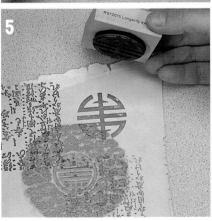

six

Remove the mask.

seven

Use contrasting ink colors.

eight

Use tracing paper to make a template the same size as the the inset panel. Use the template to cut out the panel shapes in the polymer clay. Bake the panels according to the manufacturer's instructions.

nine

Coat the inset panel with glue. Allow to dry.

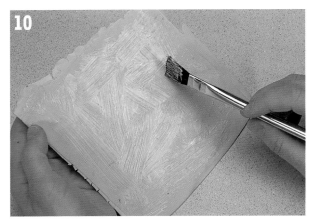

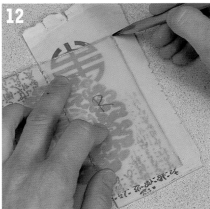

ten
Coat the veneer with glue and allow to dry.

eleven
Use the tracing paper template to guide you as you cut the veneer.

twelve
Make sure the sides will match as you cut the pieces.

thirteen
Position the veneer panels and press together. Crafter's Pic is polymer-friendly glue and acts like rubber cement when two pieces are coated and allowed to dry.

fourteen
Apply a wash of Burnt Umber paint with a soft rag to give the piece an antique look.

spirit
DOLL

Creating a doll is a great way to experiment with clay by using

stamps, textures and color. Have fun with this project, and explore

your own creative spirit.

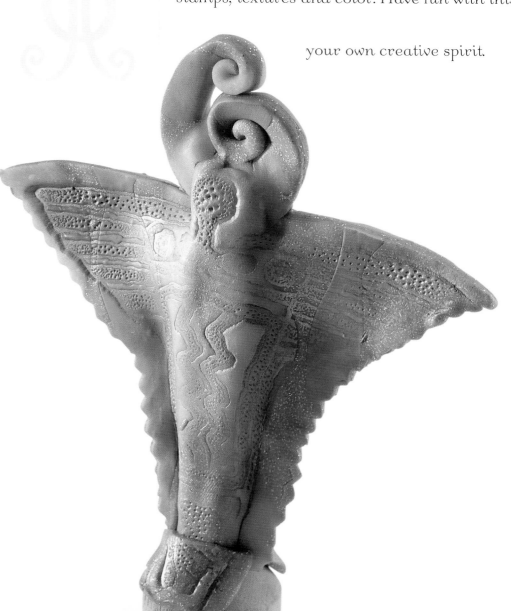

MATERIALS LIST

• wooden clothespin and stand

• tacky glue

• application brush

• white, salmon and metallic silver polymer clay

• doll stamp
  (mine is from Sherrill Kahn)

• gold pigment ink

• acrylic roller

• decorative-edge scissors

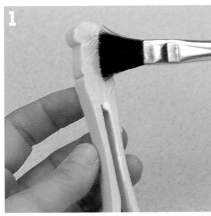

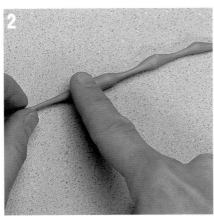

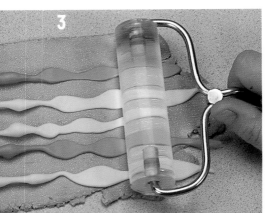

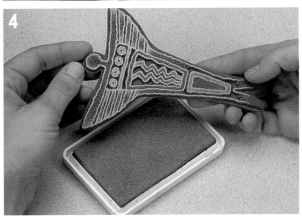

o n e

Coat the wooden clothespin and stand with glue and allow to dry.

t w o

Roll white and salmon polymer clay snakes. Make bumps in the snakes by pressing thin areas with your finger.

t h r e e

Roll a flat sheet of silver clay large enough to fit two stamped doll impressions. Roll the snakes of salmon and white clay on top of the silver clay.

f o u r

Press a doll stamp on a gold pigment inkpad.

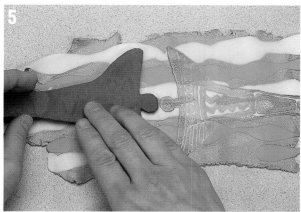

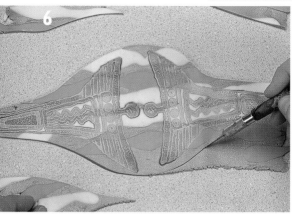

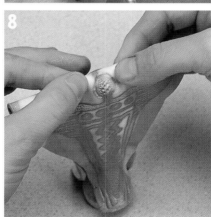

f i v e

Imprint the clay with the stamped image and flip the stamp to impress another image opposite the first. The top of the two heads should be facing each other.

s i x

Trim the sheet close to the stamp design.

s e v e n

Fold the stamped clay over the wooden pin.

e i g h t

Pinch the shoulders together.

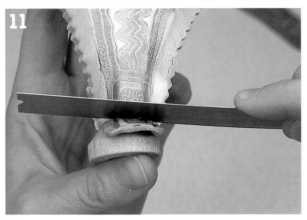

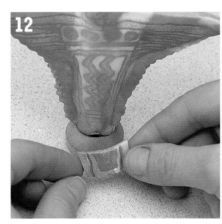

nine

Cut the area along the shoulder on each side of the head and curl into a spiral on top of the head.

ten

Pinch the sides together and cut with the decorative edge scissors.

eleven

Trim the bottom.

twelve

Place a patch of clay on the foot of the stand. Bake according to manufacturer's directions.

✳ LEAF FRAME

This frame highlights a picture of Ann and Karen's appearance on the Carol Duvall show. It was created by using impression glazing and stamped leaves filled with Liquid Sculpey.

ARTISTS: ANN AND KAREN MITCHELL,
ANKARA DESIGNS

STAMPS BY: FRIENDLY PLASTIC STAMPS

PHOTO BY: DON FELTON

✳ COVERED PAPER BOXES

These unique gift boxes were decorated with stamped and flipped impression glazing. The images were created with gold foil.

ARTISTS: ANN AND KAREN MITCHELL, ANKARA DESIGNS

STAMPS BY: STAMP HAPPY, FRIENDLY IMPRESSION AND AMACO

PHOTO BY: DON FELTON

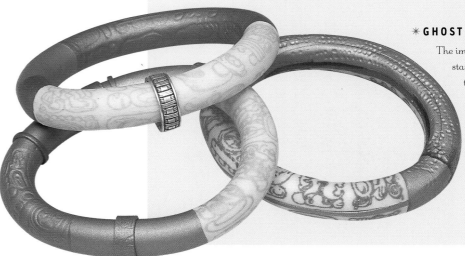

❊ GHOST BRACELETS

The images on these one-of-a-kind bracelets were stamped in pigment ink and then overlaid with translucent clay so the ink is protected from smearing.

ARTIST: BARBARA A. McGUIRE

STAMP BY: TOYBOX

PHOTO BY: DON FELTON

❊ STAMPED JOURNAL

To create this journal, templates are used to cut the stamped shapes (SEE EMBOSSED PENDANT P. 46). The collage is assembled on a sheet of clay inset into the paper journal.

ARTIST: BARBARA A. McGUIRE

STAMPS BY: LIMITED EDITION RUBBERSTAMPS

PHOTO BY: DON FELTON

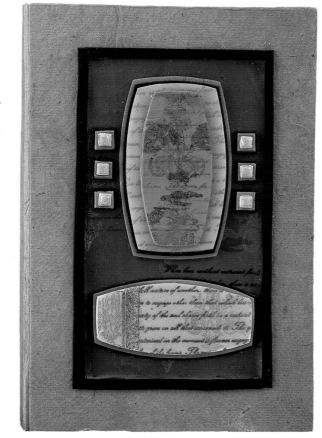

❊ BROOCH

This multicolored brooch is a pieced design of several individually stamped sheets that were cut in angled strips and arranged asymmetrically. The texture is highlighted with PearlEx pigment powder.

ARTIST: KIM KORRINGA

PHOTO BY: DON FELTON

✳ MOKUME GANE PINS

This beetle pin was etched in a tear-away transfer technique and surrounded by a stamped border. The pin is enhanced with a patina finish. The calligraphy pin was made with negative stamp images of ancient Asian calligraphy symbols.

ARTIST: NAN ROCHE

STAMP HAND-CARVED BY ARTIST

✳ SWITCH PLATE

This plate is stamped with patina-colored ink and rubbed with PearlEx powder to create a rich depth to the surface.

ARTIST: SYNDEE HOLT

STAMP BY: HERO ARTS

PHOTO BY: DON FELTON

✳ RED PENDANT

To create this pendant, an ancient image stamp was made from a drawing in clay. To finish the piece, it was antiqued with acrylic paint, sanded and buffed.

ARTIST: CAROL ZILLIACUS

STAMP HAND-CARVED BY ARTIST

✳ MASK 1

To create this unique mask, a paper form was prepared and covered by strips of dark clay with texture and pattern. After baking the mask, the strips were individually tinted with Lumiere Paints.

ARTIST: KRISTINE S. RICHARDS

STAMPS BY: ROLL A GRAPH AND CLEARSNAP

PHOTO BY: DON FELTON

✳ MASK 2

This mask was made of Premo Gold (mica shift) polymer clay. The bottom layer was stamped using a stamp by Judikins. Strips of stamped clay were appliquéd on top using a stamp by Sonlight. The entire mask was "washed" or "antiqued" with green acrylic paint and then wiped to reveal gold highlights.

ARTIST: KRISTINE S. RICHARDS

STAMPS BY: JUDIKINS AND SONLIGHT

PHOTO BY: DON FELTON

✳ FAUX IVORY BOX

This box is antiqued with acrylic paint and features letters made with a metal tool for stamping leather.

ARTIST: LINDA BERNSTEIN

✳ PRECIOUS METAL CLAY JEWELRY

This assortment of jewelry pieces have stamped polymer clay insets surrounded by precious metal clay frames.

ARTIST: LINDA BERNSTEIN

STAMPS BY: ALL NIGHT MEDIA AND THE CELTIC WORLD BY JIM POUL FOR CHRONICLE BOOKS

✳ SUN AND SPIRAL

The inside picture was stamped with clear embossing ink, then gold embossing powder was applied. The outside border squiggles were drawn with Jones Tones Plexi Glue. Jones Tones copper foils were applied to the base surface of the frame and randomly stamped with several colors of ink.

ARTIST: KRISTINE S. RICHARDS

STAMPS BY: ALL NIGHT MEDIA

PHOTO BY: DON FELTON

✳ PENDANTS

These pendants were made with gold leaf on Premo Gold clay and embellished with Chinese coins and carved jade.

ARTIST: PAT NEWTON

STAMPS BY: ALL NIGHT MEDIA AND HOT POTATOES

✳ ROUND PENDANT

This pendant has been mokume gane stamped and shaved. Blue patina finish was added and then the pendant was sanded and buffed.

ARTIST: NAN ROCHE

STAMP HAND-CARVED BY ARTIST

✳ LEATHER POUCH

This pouch with triangle stitched appliqués was made with thin clay sheets that were texture impressed and highlighted with iridescent PearlEx powder. Leather tooling stamps were used to complete the project.

ARTIST: MEREDITH ARNOLD

✳ SWITCH PLATES

These switch plates were made using various negative leaf stamps. Metallic rub-ons were also added.

ARTIST: DEBORAH ANDERSON

STAMPS BY: CREATIVE CLAYSTAMP, PENSCORE, RUBBER STAMPEDE, TOYBOX, DESIGN INNOVATIONS

✳ DRAGONFLY NECKLACE

This necklace was stamped and antiqued with white and patina color on black clay. It was then sanded and buffed.

ARTIST: EMI FUKUSHIMA

STAMP BY: HERO ARTS

✳ MYSTICAL PINS

Colorful scrap clay provided a marbled background to these gold and silver images. Sheets of clay were covered with Jones Tones transfer foils, stamped and then applied in sections.

ARTIST: KRIS RICHARDS

STAMPS BY: ALL NIGHT MEDIA

✳ CHUNKY BRACELET

This bracelet was made with a hand-carved Asian polymer stamp and Liquid Sculpey slip glaze.

ARTIST: JODY BISHEL

STAMPS HAND-CARVED BY ARTIST

✳ ALPHABET NECKLACE

This necklace was made with matching beads and then stamped and colored with PearlEx powder.

ARTIST: ALBA MONROS

STAMP BY: POSTMODERN DESIGN

✳ MINI-FRAMES

These frames were created using impression glazing and Liquid Sculpey.

ARTISTS: ANN AND KAREN MITCHELL

STAMP BY: STAMP HAPPY

✳ **HINGED FRAME (TOP)**

This frame uses hand-carved stamps with images of a spiral and a leaf, combined with acrylic paints.

ARTIST: DEBORAH ANDERSON

STAMP HAND-CARVED BY ARTIST

✳ **BARRETTES (BOTTOM)**

These barrettes were made with various stamps combined with acrylic paints.

ARTIST: DEBORAH ANDERSON

STAMPS BY: MAGIC STAMP BY PENSCORE, RUBBER STAMPEDE AND TOYBOX

* FRAMES

These two frames were created using impression glazing.

ARTISTS: ANN AND KAREN MITCHELL

STAMPS BY: STAMP HAPPY

* LEAF NECKLACE

This necklace was made with impression glazing, the stamp and flip technique, and images made with gold leaf.

ARTISTS: ANN AND KAREN MITCHELL

STAMPS BY: FRIENDLY IMPRESSION STAMPS BY AMACO

* PINCH POT

This pot was created out of faux ivory. It was made using the matrix of a self-designed stamp and antiqued with burnt sienna paint.

ARTIST: KAREN LEWIS

✳ FISH NECKLACE

A simple, elegant stamp image enhances this pendant embellished with gold leaf and beads..

ARTIST: VESTA ABEL

STAMP BY: ARTSEEDS

✳ BRACELET

The clay beads in the bead and fiber bracelet was made with a combination technique of mokume gane, stamped texture and iridescent acrylic paint.

ARTIST: LOUISE FISCHER COZZI

STAMP HAND-CARVED BY ARTIST

PHOTO BY: LOUISE FISCHER COZZI

✳ ABSTRACT BUCKLE

This buckle was created using a combination of techniques and materials including mokume gane, stamped texture, embossing powders and iridescent paint.

ARTIST: LOUISE FISCHER COZZI

STAMP HAND-CARVED BY ARTIST

PHOTO BY: MARC ROSEMBLATT

✳ POLYMER CLAY POST CARDS

These cards were made with pigment ink that is collaged on Premo clay. They can be hand-canceled at the post office and sent through the mail.

ARTIST: BARBARA MCGUIRE

STAMPS BY: LIMITED EDITION, ZETTIOLOGY, ABOVE THE MARK AND JUDIKINS

✳ JOINTED DOLL

This doll includes beaded fringe hair, copper iridescent powder, and was antiqued with acrylic paint. The stamps that were used include old wooden textile stamps, hand-carved designs, Asian chops and Chinese metal letterpress.

ARTIST: MEREDITH ARNOLD

✳ CHRISTMAS TREES

These images were stamped on Celtic-inspired Christmas trees with metallic paint and then baked. The highlights were made with metallic gel pens after baking.

ARTIST: LEIGH ROSS

STAMP BY: COMOTION

✳ SNOWFLAKES

These snowflakes were stamped with fabric ink and then baked. The highlights were created with gel markers and glitter paint.

ARTIST: LEIGH ROSS

STAMP BY: RUBBER STAMPEDE

✳ HANUKAH PIN

This pin was made on simulated ivory that was antiqued with acrylic paint.

ARTIST: LINDA BERNSTEIN

STAMP BY: ALL NIGHT MEDIA

✳ NODAWA NECKLACES

The repeated images that are held together with polymer rivets are an interesting design for these tribal necklaces. The pieces used a negative mokume gane technique and were then sanded and buffed.

ARTIST: NAN ROCHE

STAMPS BY: CREATIVE CLAYSTAMP AND HAND-CARVED STAMPS BY ARTIST

✳ PIN

This pin was made with mokume gane that was impressed with metallic powders. The zigzag design was made by impressing a pastry cutting wheel to the clay. The finishing trim on the top and the bottom of the pin is a striped cane.

ARTIST: BARBARA MCGUIRE

STAMP BY: DESIGN INNOVATIONS

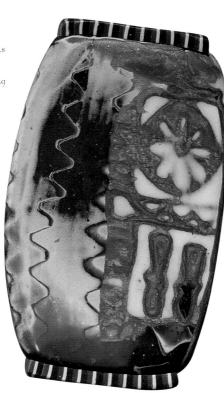

✳ GLYPH BROOCH

This brooch consists of a single stamp design created using a sanded mokume gane technique.

ARTIST: NAN ROCHE

STAMP DESIGNED BY ARTIST (READY STAMP)

* GLYPH VESSEL PENDANT

This vessel was made with the mokume gane technique and strung with attached tubes of clay.

ARTIST: NAN ROCHE

STAMP DESIGNED BY ARTIST (READY STAMP)

* EMBELLISHED TOOLS

This file and magnetic blade holder are personalized tools made with simulated bone and stone. Asian chops and Chinese metal fabric presses are used to create the images.

ARTIST: MEREDITH ARNOLD

✳ PANEL VESSEL

This vessel was made with embedded WireForm to add structure to the clay. Metallic powders serve as a release to the mokume gane stack. The color emerges as the layers are sliced.

ARTIST: BARBARA MCGUIRE

STAMP DESIGNED BY ARTIST (READY STAMP)

✳ PINS

These pins were made with Shapelets templates and heat-set with ink. Square clay punches were used to create the miniature squares. Metallic pigments highlight the edges of the composition.

ARTIST: BARABARA MCGUIRE

STAMP BY : ZETTIOLOGY

※ **RED GINKGO LEAF PENDANT**

This pendant is made using mokume gane and features a ginkgo and a leaf matrix stamp. The form was further enhanced with thin edges and additional bulk in the center of the design.

ARTIST: NAN ROCHE

STAMP DESIGNED BY ARTIST (READY STAMP)

※ **GLYPH VESSEL**

Translucent clay and gold leaf added an interesting effect when included in a mokume gane stack. The piece was made with the foil capture technique and was inspired by Tory Hughes.

ARTIST: NAN ROCHE

STAMP DESIGNED BY ARTIST (READY STAMP)

※ **DOLL PENDANT**

This abstract composition included favorite found objects. The face can be stamped or made from a mold.

ARTIST: VESTA ABEL

STAMP BY: COMOTION

✳ JAPANESE LEAF PENDANTS

These leaf pendants show the range of possibili-
ties for creating jewelry with rubberstamps
and polymer clay.

ARTIST: NAN ROCHE

STAMP DESIGNED BY ARTIST (READY STAMP)

✳ GLYPH BROOCHES

These brooches were made with negative impressions. The thin
mokume gane layers were revealed by sanding after baking and
antiqued with copper patina.

ARTIST: NAN ROCHE

STAMP DESIGNED BY ARTIST (READY STAMP)

✳ WORD POT

The texture and the use of negative space
played an important role in the design of this
beautiful pot.

ARTIST: NAN ROCHE

STAMP DESIGNED BY ARTIST (READY STAMP)

✳ LEAF PINS

These pins were stamped with formed and
shaped leaves. PearlEx powders were added for
highlight. The leaves were baked on polyster fil to support
the shape and to keep it from flattening during curing.

ARTIST: LEIGH ROSS

STAMP BY: HERO ARTS

✳ 3-D ROSE PICTURE

The stamped image on this picture is manipulated with
clay shapers and assorted modeling tools. It was highlighted with PearlEx powder.

ARTIST: LEIGH ROSS

STAMP BY: ROSEBUD RUBBER STAMPS, INC.

✳ PENDANT BLACK NECKLACE

The inner image on this pendant was designed by the artist and hand-carved. The border was stamped in silver leaf.

ARTIST: DEBBIE KRUEGER

STAMPS BY: AMERICAN ART STAMP AND
            HAND-CARVED STAMPS BY ARTIST

✳ GOLD PENDANT NECKLACE

The middle image was framed with a border and then edged in gold clay. The bead clasp was also made of clay to compliment the design.

ARTIST: DEBBIE KRUEGER

STAMPS BY: JUDIKINS AND ROLL A GRAPH

✳GEISHA MINIATURE BOOK

This book was made to simulate ivory. The stamp design emerged when it was antiqued with acrylic paint.

ARTIST: DAYLE DOROSHOW

STAMP BY: CURTIS UYEDA

✳EGYPTIAN MATCHBOX BOOK

This matchbox book was created using polymer clay, paper and acrylic paint.

ARTIST: DAYLE DOROSHOW

CONTRIBUTOR NOTES...

VESTA ABEL

P.O. Box 37041
Tucson, AZ 85740
Phone: 520-219-0407
Fax: 520-219-0559

www.artseeds.com

DEBORAH ANDERSON

265 N. 13th St.
San Jose, CA 95112
Phone: 408-998-5303

maraha@aol.com

MEREDITH ARNOLD

110 N. 201 St.
Seattle, WA 98133
Phone: 206-542-3405

marnold@nwlink.com

LINDA BERNSTEIN

ArtiQue
1001 Green Bay Rd.
Highland Park, IL 60035
Phone: 847-433-8653

www.artique.org

JODY BISHEL

548 Wakelee Ave.
Ansonia, CT 06401-1226
Phone: 203-735-5879

jbishel@aol.com

LOUISE FISCHER COZZI

419 Sixth St.
Brooklyn, NY 11215-3606
Phone: 718-499-8728
Fax: 718-499-7640

tempestal@aol.com

DAYLE DOROSHOW

Zingaro
P.O. Box 354
Fort Bragg, CA 95437
Phone: 707-962-9419

dayledoroshow@hotmail.com

EMI FUKUSHIMA

Creations By Emi
785 Sequoia Dr.
Sunnyvale, CA 94086
Phone: 408-738-1869
Fax: 408-732-4582

ecreations@aol.com

SNYDEE HOLT

180 Calla Ave.
Imperial Beach, CA 91932
Phone: 619-575-0140
Fax: 619-543-3449

syndeeh@msn.com

KIM KORRINGA

Kim Korringa Designs
156 Eldorado Dr.
Mountain View, CA 94041-2220
Phone: 650-969-7678
Fax: 650-969-1790

www.kimcreates.com

DEBBIE KREUGER

27426 Dobbin-Hufsmith Rd.
Magnolia, TX 77354
Phone: 281-356-8541
Fax: 281-259-4080

www.npcg.org/houston

KAREN LEWIS

The Spirited Bead
435 West J St.
Tehachapi, CA 93561
Phone/Fax: 661-823-1930

www.klewexpressions.com

BARBARA A. MCGUIRE

Design Innovations
P.O. Box 472334
San Francisco, CA 94147
Phone: 877-922-6366

www.claystamp.com

ANN & KAREN MITCHELL

Ankara Designs
2323 Pinecrest Dr.
Altadena, CA 91001
Phone: 626-798-8491

www.ankaradesigns.com

ALBA MONROS

211 Arbor Avenue
West Chicago, IL 60185
Phone: 630-231-8023

albasworld@interaccess.com

PAT NEWTON

924 Redwood Dr.
Danvillle, CA 94506
Phone: 925-736-4434
Fax: 925-236-4435

pnewton@sbcglobal.net

KRIS RICHARDS

Creations By Kris
1904 Viola Dr.
Ortonville, MI 48462-8886
Phone/Fax: 248-627-9517

www.creationsbykris.com

NAN ROCHE

4511 Amhesrt Rd.
Collge Park, MD 20740
Phone/Fax: 301-864-1805

www.nanroche.com

LEIGH ROSS

Polymer Clay Central
610 5th Ave.
Bradley Beach, NJ 07720
Phone: 732-776-6576

www.polymerclaycentral.com

CAROL ZILLIACUS

133303 Collingwood Terrace
Silver Spring, MD 20904-1422
Phone: 301-236-4395
Fax: 301-384-2390

carolz@concentric.net